AF341604

ECONOMIC SECURITY FOR HEALTHCARE PROVIDERS

MANAGING YOUR FINANCES FOR PROFESSIONAL & PERSONAL PROSPERITY

JOHN F. McCALLY
AND
PAUL A. WILKUS

McGraw-Hill

New York   San Francisco   Washington, D.C.   Auckland   Bogotá
Caracas   Lisbon   London   Madrid   Mexico City   Milan
Montreal   New Delhi   San Juan   Singapore
Sydney   Tokyo   Toronto

Library of Congress Cataloging–in–Publication Data

McCally, John F.
    Economic security for healthcare providers / John F. McCally and
Paul A. Wilkus.
        p.   cm.
    Includes bibliographical references and index.
    ISBN 0-07045-358-6
    1. Medicine—Practice—Finance. 2. Physicians—Finance, Personal.
I. Wilkus, Paul A.   II. Title.
R728.M336   1998
332.024´61—dc21   98-48858
                                                              CIP

McGraw-Hill

*A Division of The **McGraw·Hill** Companies*

1 2 3 4 5 6 7 8 9 0 BKM / BKM 9 0 9 8 7

ISBN 0-07045-358-6

Printed and bound by Book-Mart Press, Inc.

Cover illustration by Steve Dininno.

This publication is designed to provide accurate and authoritative
information in regard to the subject matter covered. It is sold with
the understanding that neither the author nor the publisher is engaged in rendering legal, accounting, or other professional service.
If legal advice or other expert assistance is required, the services
of a competent professional person should be sought.

*—From a Declaration of Principles jointly adopted by a Committee
of the American Bar Association and a Committee of Publishers.*

PREFACE

As described in author John McCally's last book, *Capitation for Physicians,* the economic realities of the business of medicine require physicians today to understand where their practice revenues come from (i.e., contracts) and how to keep as much of that revenue as possible. *Economic Security for Healthcare Providers* is designed to help physicians who are dealing with those economic realities improve the financial side of their practice. Such improvement, the authors believe, will be achieved by the practices using appropriate strategic planning and operations and wisely investing their resulting revenues in such a manner that they create economic security for both their practice and personal financial future.

This book is intended to serve as the basis for understanding and carrying out future discussions with your professional advisors. Great effort has been taken to provide accurate numbers and explanations. However, the information in this book should not be relied on for the preparation of tax returns or investment decisions. As most everyone in the United States knows, the interpretation and impact of the Balanced Budget Act passed by Congress and signed by the President in 1997 will create differences for individuals and professional corporations, which will often create a need for professional advice, certainly given the differences in state laws and changing IRS regulations. Assumed rates of return are not in any way to be taken as a guaranteed projection of the actual return from any recommended investment opportunity. Similarly, the actual application of some of this book's concepts and recommendations may need to have proper tax/legal counsel advice.

The authors of this book have worked with physicians and healthcare providers for more than fifty years collectively. They are well aware that many physicians today are working considerably harder than they were five to ten years ago. They also recognize as they assist physicians and medical groups today that the decreasing reimbursement that most physicians have been receiving for their services in the last five to ten years is not going to stabilize. In fact, particularly with the Balanced Budget Act of 1997 having such a major impact on Medicare, the authors, like most physicians today, are well aware that Medicare reimbursement for many physician services will likely be decreasing over the next five years.

The author's goal in writing this book is to help those physicians who identify with the above conditions prepare for and successfully work through the changes that will be directly impacting their financial growth from both their medical practices, as well as personal finances. Based on their experience, the authors have developed the first half of this book, primarily authored by John McCally, to address practice financial management issues, and the second half, primarily authored by Paul Wilkus, to pertain to personal financial issues.

ACKNOWLEDGMENTS

Both authors would like to acknowledge their clients and professional associates for the opportunity over the last three decades to learn from and share with information that improves financial security for physicians and healthcare providers. The authors would also like to acknowledge the love, support, and patience of our families during this seemingly long writing and publication process, as well as the understanding and assistance of Kris Rynne and Tom Sharpe at McGraw-Hill.

CONTENTS

How to Take Control of Your Practice Contracts with Managed Care Companies

There are more than 650 HMOs and 1,000 PPOs in the United States. In addition to the HMOs and PPOs, there is a growing number of business coalitions and large employers who are directly contracting with physicians, medical groups, and other provider organizations. In many cases, there are hundreds of physician hospital organizations (PHOs), independent physician organizations (IPOs), and management service organizations (MSOs) who contract with physicians and medical groups as providers and then in turn contract with third party payors. The federal government, through Health Care Finance Administration (HCFA), and many state governments are both encouraging and requiring Medicare and Medicaid recipients to enter "managed care" arrangements that include contracts with physicians and medical groups. The sum and substance of all of the above organizations and their activity with physicians is that the care of patients in the future will be almost completely provided through contracts. Therefore, physicians and their practice administrators/managers in the future must become knowledgeable contract negotiators and plan administrators to have a practice that is financially successful.

Assuming this is correct, the challenge for physicians in the future will be to understand managed care contracts through appropriate analysis of the key issues, particularly reimbursement and financial risk. Equally important is how to negotiate and then implement a variety of types of contracts. Often, even with the same HMO or PPO, there will be different contract clauses for individual physicians/physician groups depending on who the managed care organization has contracted with to be the third party payor. Recognizing that if you've seen one managed care contract, you have seen one managed care contract, it is important to treat each contract individually. Similarly, it is important to recognize that negotiations with individual representatives from the various managed care organizations (MCOs) will also take a unique approach depending on each individual negotiator, his or her role in that organization's management hierarchy, and the total approach of MCOs to using their contracts with providers to improve their bottom line.

CONTRACT ANALYSIS

Each contract physicians and medical groups receive will undoubtedly have different clauses in them, so it is imperative to look at each and every clause in a contract during the analysis stage. MCOs and their negotiators send a contract to physicians, or deliver it to their practices and often provide the following information, "We're about to sign a large employer group and if you and your practice want to be included among the providers available for their employees, you need to sign this contract immediately and return it to us by the end of the week." This is an example of a negotiation tactic of MCOs. It cannot be emphasized enough that regardless of the time deadline that is perceived as important, more important is the need to first thoroughly analyze the contract. The book by author McCally, *Capitation for Physicians,* goes into much greater detail on the analysis of contracts and provides a list of fifty key questions to ask the MCO to gain a better understanding of the contract. Here, the essential areas of a contract that physicians and managers need to analyze before making a commitment to the MCO are reviewed.

The first area that needs to be explored thoroughly is the actual services that the company is requesting physicians to provide. Often, a contract will call for "typical" services provided by this type of practice (e.g., cardiology, ob-gyn, primary care). Unfortunately, when it comes to reimbursement, there are often differences of opinion between the MCOs and providers relating to what are "typical" services. Therefore, it is strongly recommended that each contract has a specific list of service CPT codes and their descriptions either as a part of a contract or an attachment.

The next area that needs specific attention is the type of reimbursement for those specific services. That section should be followed by an analysis of the method of payment for that kind of reimbursement (i.e., if it's capitation, when is the monthly per-member-per-month [PMPM] check sent from the MCO to the physician/physician group?). Next, particularly if the contract is capitated, the numbers of patients to be capitated should be defined, with a demographic description of those patients that includes at least the patient's age, sex, and zip code.

Many of the newer managed care contracts are calling for the provider to submit outcomes results, making it important to determine, if such a clause is in the contract, the format for such reports and the frequency of such reports. Many physicians/medical groups currently do not have the computer systems that can generate the types of outcomes reports being requested in contracts. To prepare those reports manually is extremely expensive and time-consuming and maybe not even possible without an appropriate management information system (MIS) system. Next are the other types of report requirements that the MCO is often requesting in the contract as "typical" financial data. Many physicians would interpret this terminology to refer to patient claims when, in fact, the MCO can be requesting financial data from the provider practice that often goes beyond routine claims reporting and gets into practice management accounting results.

The next area of the contract that needs to be well understood is the geographic location of the patient population and the requirements of the MCO to providers for servicing those patients within a "reasonable driving distance." If the service area includes multiple counties and the MCO anticipates that their patients will need service within a "reasonable driving time" (i.e., fifteen minutes), it may require the providers who sign such contracts to open satellite offices in counties other than their current location. Although this may sound reasonable, in some cases even attractive, the cost of providing care in a satellite office may far exceed the actual number of patients who seek care at that office under such a contract.

The next major consideration is the need to change or upgrade the practice computer system to be "on-line" with the MCO regarding the MCO's patient verification process. Particularly with capitation, it is important to know which patients are still being included by the MCO in the monthly capitation check to the practice. Similarly, when patients show up who no longer are covered by their former employer's policy, the provider needs to have assurance that the MCO has an accurate and valid listing of patients so that the providers are not caring for patients that the MCO is going to deny reimbursement for during a given month.

Next the contract, particularly if it is a capitated contract, should address stop-loss provisions and settlement of payment disputes. Finally, among the key areas to initially be analyzed in any contract is the providing of the medical services to patients covered under the contract through the emergency room (ER) or "out of area." These two specific areas can be very costly to the providers if they are financially responsible for care of such patients but do not provide it either in the ER or out of area.

DEVELOPING YOUR NEGOTIATING STRATEGY

Particularly with MCOs and in a competitive environment, it is important to understand where the MCO is coming from when they present you with a contract. Although there may be differences between HMOs (nonprofit versus for-profit) and PPOs (physician-owned versus hospital-owned versus for-profit), most MCOs are in the end looking to increase their bottom line through contracting with providers. *Most MCOs are acutely aware of the need to reduce total medical expenditures to help increase their bottom line.* Even nonprofit MCOs want to increase their "reserves," which allows them to be more competitive in the years when they are lowering their premium rates to capture greater market share. Other key "global" needs of MCOs include having their enrollees surveyed with a positive satisfaction rate and meeting annual projections for all phases of their operations.

These global objectives often get translated differently in the form of clauses in provider contracts. This is certainly true with physicians/medical group contracts because the physicians are the ultimate individuals responsible for ordering tests, services, and hospitalizations for MCOs enrollees. In addition to these global objectives of the MCOs, there are often specific needs or goals of the MCO, depending on a specific marketplace and the competitive nature of that marketplace. All of this is background information necessary to help you develop your contract negotiation strategy relating to a specific MCO contract.

Physicians and medical groups must put their managed care contracting into a specific perspective relating to their practice. It is essential to understand where your practice's revenue is currently coming from and what it costs the practice to receive those patients/revenues from different sources (e.g., in some locations, Medicare reimbursement is not only low but costly to bill and collect, whereas in other locations today, Medicare reimbursement is very desirable and, in some cases, greater than other payors). Therefore, knowing your own patient mix and cost of providing care to various types of patients is a major prerequisite to evaluating a new contract. Once you have determined that the MCO is a company you want to have as a "partner" and that their current/projected patients are appropriate for your practice, it is time to develop a negotiation strategy relating to the contract that they have presented. Emphasis has been placed on the term *partner* because we believe that there will be a long-term relationship between the provider and the MCO over a period far exceeding an initial one-year contract. The foundation then of negotiating a successful contract initially, and in subsequent years renewing that contract, should help put the contract into a perspective of how to develop a winning relationship for both the MCO and you as the provider/organization.

Other background information that is helpful in developing your contract strategy is to know the number of other physicians in your service area that provide the same type of care. Then determine whether the MCO is offering all other similar providers the same contract or whether you and your practice have an opportunity for an "exclusive" arrangement of some type. If it is not an exclusive contract, it is important to determine, if possible, how other providers both in and out of your geographic service area are being paid for similar services. At that point, you need to determine whether that reimbursement covers your cost of providing those services.

If you have the opportunity to enter into a "partnership" arrangement with the MCO, part of your strategy should be to determine whether there can be incentives built into your contract for providing quality care at cost-effective rates. This may be particularly important should the acceptance of a large influx of patients and MCO requirements mean a change in the way patients are treated or require additional costs (i.e., a new computer system will be added to the practice).

PREPARATION FOR NEGOTIATION SESSIONS

Assuming you have analyzed the proposed contract from the MCO and determined that you want to "partner" with the MCO, and further assuming that you have determined your advantages and potential disadvantages from the proposed contract, it is now time to prepare to actually negotiate that contract and determine the best ways to achieve your goals in the process. The term *process* is used because the first negotiation session with a new MCO should be only the first step in the process. Before the initial session, you should select the appropriate members of your negotiating team. It is fairly safe to assume that the initial session may be only with a "director of provider relations" or "manager of contract relations." Whatever the individual's title, it is important to determine before the meeting whether others from the MCO will be in attendance. Often, this will mean not only the initial "provider relations representative" but also someone from the MCO's finance division and someone from the legal division. Depending on the type of contract and how large it may be, the medical director and/or administrator of the HMO may be present. In any event, at each negotiation session in the process, you should determine who will attend the meeting from the MCO and from your practice so that you can plan to have an equal number of individuals on your side of the negotiation table. At a minimum, it is recommended that at every meeting, the president/managing partner of the medical practice be there with the practice administrator/manager. Depending on who comes from the MCO, you may want to add additional members from your group (i.e., your utilization management director or medical director if you have one, as well as someone who is particularly experienced with negotiating managed care contracts).

Before the first negotiation session, determine with your partners, if necessary, who has the authority on your side to sign the contract and at what level of reimbursement for specific services. At the same time, determine whether the representatives from the MCO at any given meeting are the representatives who have the authority to sign a negotiated contract. Often, even with a "standard" contract, the individual from the MCO who attends the initial meeting will not have the authority to sign that contract. He or she may ask you to sign the contract and then offer to "take it back for appropriate signatures and return a signed copy to you."

Last, before you go into any contract negotiation session, prepare an agenda for the meeting that is favorable to your particular approach, have a prepared list of questions for the MCO, and have assigned specific responsibilities to members of your team (i.e., one person to be the primary spokesperson, one person to take notes of what is said/agreed to, and one person whose primary responsibility is to attentively listen to what both sides say). This is often important as in the process of negotiating, the main spokesperson is concentrating on what to say and how to say it and it is therefore important to have an "objective" listener who can provide feedback to you and your team after the session as to what was said and implied by both sides.

THE NEGOTIATION SESSIONS

Assuming that you and your negotiating team are prepared as recommended, which includes having an agenda, the actual sessions themselves should be relatively straightforward. The meetings should usually be held at alternate sites for each session, and depending on the size and importance of the contract, a neutral site may be chosen for what is likely to be last session. At what is considered to be the last session, the decision maker and signer for both organizations should be in attendance. For the sessions before the "final session," the note taker should prepare written notes of what was agreed to and/or discussed and what will be the agenda items for the next session. The "minutes" of previous meetings should be sent to all participants and kept in a notebook that is brought by the note taker to each session for quick reference.

As the old saying goes, "Timing is everything." This is particularly true with contract negotiations. Usually, the managed care organizations have some marketing/sales deadlines that they want to meet. Similarly, most physician organizations have their own critical needs that may pertain to patient care being given to current patients and not trying to unnecessarily stress out a very busy practice. In general, however, it is usually best at the first negotiating session to determine a specific timetable for the total process. This is important for two reasons: (1) the marketplace environment may change if the contract negotiations are prolonged, effecting either the MCO or the provider group, and (2) particularly with larger MCOs, their representatives' job responsibilities and location may change, creating a potential new dynamic to the process. This almost always elongates the process, and there will often be operational issues within a medical practice that need to be changed to implement a new contract. It is helpful from a planning standpoint for the physicians and administrator/practice manager to have a sense as soon as possible when the contract may be concluded from a negotiation standpoint and at what point will it be implemented.

WHAT IS YOUR VALUE?

From the initial negotiation session through the last session, it is important to understand the positives about your particular practice/medical group and how the MCO values those positives. Your organization may have a long-standing reputation, an excellent location, proven quality outcomes, proven cost-effectiveness, and/or all of these. However, the positive aspects of your practice must be communicated correctly and appropriately to match the needs of the MCOs and their perception of your organization's contribution of those positive aspects of your practice in the marketplace. Assuming a good match exists, the value of your practice may be reflected in higher contract reimbursement.

WILL THIS CONTRACT INCREASE YOUR BOTTOM LINE?

It should go without saying that all of the items described previously relating to managed care contract negotiation are extremely important in helping to end the process with an increase to your bottom line. However, there are many more items that are also important, including many more details and aspects of appropriate contract strategy and negotiation that whole books are written about. For those physicians who have not participated in the process before, there are not only books but also seminars that can prove helpful in gaining a better understanding about how to achieve your contracting goals. With that in mind, remember one final word of advice: *Never sign a contract that will have a negative impact on your cash flow.* This is something that can be included in your initial discussions with the MCO/MCO negotiator. Make it clear that your practice cannot accept any contract that has a negative impact on your cash flow. In that way, the MCO, if it truly wants to contract with you and be a "partner" for some time, will understand that it, as well as you and your organization, need to have not only a positive contract but an underlying philosophy of "partnership." You also need the accounting and management information systems tools and/or reports to ensure that your common goals are met.

SHIFTING OF FINANCIAL RISK

As the trend in healthcare is for more and more mergers and larger physician organizations/networks, so is the continued trend toward larger managed care contracts with a shifting of financial risk to providers. In general, as physician practices merge and grow, they in essence become multimillion dollar practices. Such practices need to have a focus not only on providing quality care to their patients but also on running effectively as a business. Such a change in philosophy is often needed for physician organizations to ensure that their managed care risk and capitation contracts do not negatively impact their bottom line.

As part of operating their nonmedical activities as a business, medical groups and physician organizations today need to have the business systems, accounting, and computer capabilities that make other multimillion dollar businesses successful. This is particularly true of every business that is primarily a contractually oriented business. Contracts, especially in the healthcare industry usually run for one to three years. Therefore, at the end of each contractual period, you as the provider of the service and the receiver of reimbursement for that service need to know whether you made or lost money on that contract. Then you need to decide whether to renew that contract or not to contract with that MCO in the future. If you decide to renew the contract in the future, you need to have the results of the financial variables of the contract well understood. Then in the next negotiation process, you can specify your goals for the next contractual period and negotiate accordingly. As more financial risk is shifted to physicians in the future, the bottom line of your practice will be increased or decreased depending on how well you negotiate all parts of future contracts.

Increasing Cash Flow through Improving Operations

In Chapter 1, the importance of maximizing revenue through the contracting process was discussed. However, maximizing revenues and increasing revenues are not always the same. With managed care companies charging an average of 12 to 18% for their administrative and management costs, the dollars available for providers of healthcare services through managed care contracts are bound to be lower and lower as the managed care environment becomes more and more competitive. Employers across the United States, either by coalitions or by direct contracting, want to reduce their employee healthcare costs. Therefore, they are asking managed care companies to maintain level, or reduce, their premium charges while simultaneously asking for higher quality outcomes. In turn, those managed care companies that are getting "squeezed" are trying to "squeeze" the providers with whom they contract.

For most physicians, with some exceptions such as pediatricians and pediatric subspecialists, most of the revenue from any one single source is usually coming from Medicare. Therefore, it is of particular importance for those practices who want to increase their cash flow to offset the projected decreasing revenues from Medicare.

Two major events that occurred in the second half of 1997 are of concern to many providers of healthcare services today because of their potential ramifications, particularly for Medicare providers for years to come. Those two events are the indictment of Columbia/HCA management for numerous illegal activities, involving fraudulent billing of Medicare. The second major event is the release by the Office of the Inspector General, Department of Health and Human Services, of its first full-scale audit results. The initial results of this first full-scale audit (potentially to be done annually) was the revelation of an estimated $23 billion in improper payments made under Medicare fee-for-service in 1996. Interestingly, this $23 billion in improper payments if eliminated every year for five years equals the proposed $115 billion savings estimated through the Balanced Budget Act of 1997 signed by President Clinton to take place over the years 1998 through 2002 (data from Congressional Record).

All of the $23 billion was not improper payments to physicians. In fact, the estimated percentage of improper payments to physicians equaled approximately 22% of the total $23 billion. Of particular interest in the Inspector General's report were the following types of billing errors that resulted in certain payments to physicians in 1996:

- Lack of medical necessity: $614 million
- Insufficient documentation: $1.94 billion
- No documentation: $816 million
- Incorrect coding: $1.70 billion

Unfortunately, the bad news from that audit report does not stop there. The Congressional House Health Subcommittee General Counsel Harriet Rabb recently conceded that part B billing by teaching physicians "have not been consistently and clearly articulated" over several decades. Questionable billing practices by academic physicians are currently the subject of a controversial fraud enforcement audit unrelated to the Inspector General's audit recently released. Ms. Rabb indicated that there are "no easy solutions" for physicians, warning that the new audit report findings may "only encourage more heavy-handed enforcement activities." A similar warning of potential bad news for Medicare providers has come from a high ranking Democrat, Representative Pete Stark (CA). He said the audit indicated that neither HCFA nor its private contracts "have the structure or the resources to deal with all of the criminals who see the Medicare program as an easy target." He further stated, "It's the providers who are not doing their job," and federal policy makers should "make it very expensive for them if they don't keep adequate records."

All of this is not good news for the business of healthcare providers. Coding and documentation for services has become increasingly more complex over the last decade, particularly with Medicare billing. As Medicare billing became more complex and was often submitted electronically to the Medicare intermediary, many physician practices and medical groups determined that they needed to have a "coding clerk." Unfortunately the complexities of the system, and often a lack of good communication and medical documentation by providers, has created a situation where a coding clerk is often not sufficient to maximize reimbursement appropriately and to avoid Medicare billing audits in the future. Statements such as those by General Counsel Rabb and Congressman Stark are extremely disconcerting. However, they are nowhere near as disconcerting as going through a Medicare audit itself. For a physician's office, its staff, and its physician providers, a Medicare audit, even one that returns a clean bill of health (very unlikely) is still time-consuming, costly, and often emotionally draining on physicians and their staff. The Inspector General's Office (OIG) indicated in its audit report that it was unable to specify which medical specialties were more involved in the inappropriate payments. However, the OIG has provided HCFA with a "detailed list of certain procedure codes that have a high frequency of error." At present, that list has not been shared with physician providers. The audit did offer a number of examples. Two such examples include the following: (1) medical records for ten physician visits during a patient's hospital stay did not contain support for eight of the sessions, indicating a $386 overpayment, and (2) a payment for an echocardiography interpretation was inappropriate because medical records from a cardiology consultation several weeks earlier indicated that no further follow-up was necessary.

Many physicians and practice managers reading the previous examples would indicate to Congressman Stark and HCFA that if their offices had made those particular errors that this was not a situation of attempting to "steal more money from Medicare coffers" as Congressman Stark has indicated but were more likely honest errors on the part of a billing clerk/physician providers who were overworked, understaffed, or not fully informed of how best to complete a full billing with appropriate documentation to the Medicare intermediary. In the United States during the last five years, there has been a significant increase in mergers, management service organizations (MSOs), growing group practices, and physician practice management companies. One major factor for these changes toward larger organizations and medical integration is the potential for improving the billing and collection function of every practice.

Regardless of whether a physician practice today remains solo or a small single specialty, or whether it merges and increases in size to a large group practice that has billings of more than $20 million a year, the need for increased experienced staffing, training, internal audits, and new billing/management information systems all seem to be necessary to meet Medicare billing requirements. Hopefully, most physician practices will not be audited, although there has been speculation that the Inspector General cases against the large organizations like Columbia/HCA will result in large fines/settlements that will be used in part or whole to fund an ever-increasing scope of Medicare billing fraud. What we know for sure is that the FBI is running medical care fraud hot line advertisements in the press. Whether the speculation about Columbia/HCA is true or not, the physicians of today can improve their practices' cash flow either through internal activities or by hiring outside expertise to meet the ever-changing Medicare billing requirements. Physicians need to accept the responsibility to document appropriately, as well as to have billing and collection staffs who perform their jobs appropriately. In larger practices, this oversight can be accomplished by coding evaluations and audits, done by objective third party organizations and, in some cases, educational programs put on by national medical specialty organizations, as well as HCFA itself. It should be recognized that with the rapid growth of HMOs and PPOs, most medical practices also need to increase the expertise and capability of their billing staffs to handle the difference and complexities of MCO billing and collection.

Each practice can significantly increase its cash flow if the billing is done correctly the first time. Often, MCOs or Medicare intermediaries return claims to physician provider practices indicating denial of those claims, sometimes for one reason and sometimes for multiple reasons. In some very busy practices, such denials are accepted as the gospel truth. In other offices, the Medicare denials are often researched and resubmitted on appeal to Medicare with what is hoped to be adequate documentation for appropriate payment. In either event, cash flow can be significantly increased if the claim is submitted correctly the first time. It is recommended here that physician practices have a Medicare committee made up of at least one physician and one nurse, as well as someone from the collection office who routinely reviews Medicare denials and follow-up appeals. In addition, it is important for the practices that believe that they have been getting a large number of denials from Medicare to research a group of denials and physically take those denials with new documentation to the appropriate department in the office of the Medicare intermediary in their state. Person-to-person contact and obvious willingness on the part of the physician office to improve its billing accuracy will enable that practice to increase its cash flow from its Medicare billings. It should go without saying, however, that it is also important to realize that such activity devoted to the billing and collection function of non-Medicare patient services will equally provide an increased cash flow to each practice that makes the additional investment necessary to meet the third party payor requirements in an accurate and timely fashion. We anticipate more and more seniors in Medicare, and for some medical specialties, there may be a greater percentage of Medicare patients in their practice; for them, it is going to be extremely important to concentrate on improving effectiveness of their ongoing Medicare changes in billing requirements and reimbursement.

As the complexity of billing and collection becomes a greater factor in the economic success of a practice, regardless of the economic trends and activity in the service area of any given practice, physicians must concentrate on two key factors to improve their cash flow: (1) the number of employees in the practice and (2) the productivity and results of those employees. As mentioned earlier, a multimillion dollar medical practice may have somewhat different services and procedures for getting paid for those services but, in essence, that practice is a multimillion dollar business. The number of workers and their productivity are keys to increasing cash flow. Many hospitals in the United States, as their bed occupancy has decreased, have downsized their employee staff. This is not to suggest that every practice should downsize. In fact, one large single specialty medical group was particularly proud of the low overhead that they had achieved. They were to be commended because they were definitely lower in overhead than almost all other medical groups of the same size in the same specialty. However, they had achieved such a low overhead by keeping their number of employees to a bare minimum, making patient services the primary focus of the physicians and somewhat limited employee staff. Unfortunately what happened to that group was that their accounts receivable kept growing to the point of being extremely high for a group of their size, primarily because they did not have an adequate staff to focus on their billing and collection activity. A better arrangement would be to periodically have an effective internal or external benchmarking review of employee staffing and productivity. Such reviews can be seen either as threatening from a moral standpoint to employees or, if done appropriately, as an opportunity to reward highly effective employees. Again, the purpose of this recommendation is to help physicians and their practices focus on ways to increase their cash flow. This will not happen without a focus on all aspects of the practice, including the physician services and the numbers of employees, their capabilities, and their productivity.

The healthcare industry today is unfortunately on a collision course between two highly important trends. The first one has been discussed at some length; that is, the fact that the regulators of Medicare and Medicaid and other governmental programs are basically going to be doing what they can to reduce reimbursement to healthcare providers. On the other hand, in many areas of the United States, we are seeing a shortage of experienced and skilled workers who can assist physicians in their practices to become cost-effective. Similar to what the manufacturing and automobile industries went through in the last several decades, the healthcare industry of the twenty-first century must be aware of its total cost and how to use modern technology to become as cost-effective as possible. Like other industries, the healthcare industry, including practices of medicine, will in the future need to "invest" in modern technology (i.e., new computer systems and well-trained competent personnel who can help the physician providers maximize and increase their cash flow).

3

CHAPTER

Understanding Your Non-HMO Contracts and Their Potential Financial Impact on Total Practice Revenues

As indicated in Chapter 1, it is likely that healthcare in the future will basically be delivered almost totally under contractual situations, which is why so much emphasis has been placed on preparing the business side of each practice and medical group to meet the changing financial challenges of often being a multimillion dollar business. However, in addition to the importance of revenue-producing contracts, as is true with many other businesses, there is an ever-increasing amount of contract activities that become part of the daily life of your business of medicine.

Understanding these contracts is extremely important because today *there seems to be a growing trend toward litigation— a trend that is likely to continue into the future.* Suits are filed daily in the courts against many businesses, no matter what the size, including medical businesses. Losing a business suit might create such a financial hardship on the practice that it would negate the hard work and good patient care provided by the practice's physicians over years of caring for their patients. Therefore, it is important to point out various aspects of the contractual side of business and explain how physicians may protect their practice and revenues.

For years, physicians have been told by insurance companies, managed care companies, and risk management companies that they must document their patient findings and recommendations. The same is true of business dealings. It is extremely important to have written confirmation of verbal agreements that physicians/practice owners and their practice managers develop with vendors, employees, and physician partners. By keeping written documentation of such verbal agreements, the practice gives the other person (e.g., a vendor or employee) a chance to agree on the written interpretation. This is extremely important from a legal defense standpoint should a lawsuit ever develop. Such written documentation not only is important in the defense aspects of a trial but can potentially eliminate the willingness of the other side to take a grievance to court.

It is important to recognize a contract in today's litigious environment is a legally enforceable agreement. Such a contract requires an offer, an acceptance of the offer, and consideration of some type. Contracts can be verbal but are usually written. Certain types of contracts in business must be in writing: contracts for the sale of goods that have a value of more than $500, contracts for the sale of land, contracts that cannot be performed within one year, and contracts to pay another's debt. Because this chapter is not meant to be "legal advice" but rather business and financial advice, it is necessary to point out that there are some types of contracts that the courts will not enforce. Examples of those unenforceable contracts include those with some type of act prohibited by law or an agreement to engage in discriminatory conduct.

EMPLOYEE-RELATED CONTRACTS

Employment Contracts

Two other issues are extremely important: employment contracts and employee policies. Let's first talk about hiring new physicians and offering them an employment contract. Assuming that the prospective physician has visited the practice and there seems to be a good, positive relationship potential, it is important to provide a written offer of employment to the candidate. The proposed contract will help clarify any misunderstandings between the candidate and the practice. It will also be helpful in the future should there be any reason for either side to change their agreement or enforce a certain part of the agreement. For physicians coming out of a residency program or coming out of a first-time practice situation, their understanding of issues such as restrictive practice covenants or partnership tracks will often be best understood if the candidate has an opportunity to study the written offer, which should include explanations of new terminology such as restricted covenants. Physicians who come to work under an assumed understanding and later find that they misunderstood verbal comments made by the practice are often unhappy physicians, which can affect how they care for patients.

Most practices will usually want to confer with their own legal counsel when developing employment contracts because all states have somewhat different legislation and regulations pertaining to the typical clauses that are in business contracts and sometimes even toward specifics of medical employment contracts. Terms such as restricted covenants are not found in other business contracts. Hopefully, your attorney can give you suggestions to keep the contract as relatively straightforward and understandable as possible, given the legalese that a state law might normally require for such contracts.

Not only must key legal aspects and state law requirements be included in employment contracts, but also *there should be a definite description of how new physicians will be paid, when they will be paid, and when that pay might change.* A standard sentence relating to this subject might be as follows: "The new physician will be paid $120,000 per year at the rate of $10,000 per month, payable on the last business day of each month, and this arrangement will not change until the earliest of two events; that is, the generation by said physician of $300,000 in net revenue *collected* or sometime during month thirteen of employment when the physician will be given his or her first annual performance evaluation, which could lead to a salary increase."

Similarly, should the physician be hired with the assumption that he or she will be a full partner at some point in the future, such an offer should include specifics such as follows: "After three years of employment, assuming satisfactorily annual evaluations for the three years, the newly employed physician will become a full partner in the practice upon arranging for his or her share of ownership in the practice to be paid for in a satisfactorily manner to the then-current practicing partners." Some contracts will then go on to state that the current method for new physicians to buy in to the practice is plan A or plan B but that in month thirty-seven, there could be other options as well. Last, it is important to indicate how long the employment contract offer is valid. Sometimes this is simply a formality, but in other situations, the candidate may be considering other offers and/or the practice may have other candidates that they may wish to make an offer.

Many readers will understand the importance of what has been said about physician employment agreements. It is important to recognize that there are other types of contracts commonly used in medical business that also need to be handled professionally and adhered to by all parties. Other types of contracts include agreements to purchase supplies, insurance agreements, service agreements, confidentiality agreements, noncompete agreements, and agreements to buy or sell real estate.

Employee Policies

As mentioned earlier, *the employee handbook becomes a type of legal contract between physician owners as employers and their employees.* As an example of an important part of an employee handbook, it is helpful for physician owners/employers to know about one of the key aspects of employment lawsuits today—sexual harassment. In 1980, the Equal Employment Opportunities Commission issued federal guidelines declaring sexual harassment an unlawful employment practice. The Supreme Court decision in 1986, *Meritor v Vinton,* affirmed these guidelines and the fact that harassment on the basis of sex is illegal.

Although sexual harassment has been defined and declared illegal, several problems concerning prevention and handling of sexual harassment continue at all levels of employment today.

Whether there is confirmation in the courts or not, a sexual harassment lawsuit is definitely a bad situation for physician owners/employers, their employees, and the public, including their patients. Because sexual harassment is often defined as an inappropriate use of power that can create hostile work environments, it is important that the medical "business" have as part of their handbook a section on sexual harassment, what the philosophy is of the organization toward sexual harassment in the workplace and inclusion of key phrases such as "unacceptable when any unwanted, unwelcome or unsolicited sexual conduct is imposed on a person who regards it as offensive and undesirable." This type of definition of key phrases needs to be clear to all employees, including all physician owners/physicians. *There should also be a grievance procedure outlined that indicates to the employees how to report any unwanted or unwelcome behavior.* The reporting of a complaint should lead to an investigation procedure as also outlined in the employee handbook. Unfortunately, complaints and lawsuits regarding sexual harassment have immediate consequences, much like a Medicare audit of billing and collection practices. The time and effort to prepare for either a Medicare audit or sexual harassment lawsuit are immense, and there is a definite increase in morale problems, as well as potentially a decrease in patient visits once such a lawsuit is public knowledge. Therefore, the recommendation is that your sexual harassment policy should be reviewed by an expert, included in your employee handbook, and referred to, often as a means to prevent both sexual harassment and resulting lawsuits.

REAL ESTATE PURCHASES AND LEASES

One of the most common contractual arrangements for medical practices is related to real estate purchases and leases. In most states, oral arrangements relating to real estate and leases are unenforceable. In fact, most states require that real estate transactions be in writing and use very complex legalese. Real estate or real property consists of land, buildings, and fixtures to the land and buildings, as opposed to personal property, which can be considered portable. Should a physician or a medical practice want to acquire a first office or a new satellite office, such an acquisition can take place through an actual purchase, contract for deed or lease.

Because at some point most medical organizations need space to provide care for their patients, it seems appropriate to provide some brief pointers relating to how these transactions can best be achieved. The purchase of real estate usually occurs through the use of a purchase agreement, which basically is a contract to purchase such real estate at a future date. The future date is when the actual transfer of ownership takes place. A purchase agreement, sometimes called a contract of sale or an earnest money contract, is used for recording the agreement between the buyer and the seller of key items such as the agreed-on price, the date of the transfer of ownership, and the identification of any conditions or responsibilities that need to be resolved before the closing date. At the closing, there needs to be evidence that the seller can convey legal title to the purchaser. This is done through a deed, which must be in writing to be enforceable. The deed must identify the parties involved as well as the real estate/land. It must be signed by the seller and state a present intent to convey ownership. A "warranty" deed contains various assurances about the transaction, such as there are no encumbrances to the property. In contrast, a "quit claim" deed expressly states that it makes no warranty. The seller simply conveys whatever interest in the property it possesses. Following the conveyance by deed, the title should be promptly recorded, usually at a courthouse.

As part of such transactions, title insurance is often recommended or required. Title insurance is an insurance policy that protects the lender if title defects are found after the closing. Most lenders require such insurance as a condition of the mortgage loan. Title insurance can also be purchased to protect the real estate purchaser. Title insurance protects against hidden defects in the chain of ownership, such as forgeries or misdescriptions of property.

In many cases, particularly for new providers in the marketplace, acquiring property through a lease is financially a more palatable transaction. Legally, a lease provides possession of the property in exchange for periodic lease payments. Unless there is a purchase option included in the lease, there is no transfer of ownership. Basically, a lease must be in writing to be enforceable. A purchase option, if included, is essentially an irrevocable offer by the landlord to sell the property to the tenant. Such options usually have time deadlines, and if the tenant fails to meet such deadlines, the purchase option becomes unenforceable. Normally, a lease will describe conditions that constitute default by the tenant, allowing the landlord to terminate the lease and re-enter the property. Such acts of default include failure to pay rent and abandonment of the premises. Under most leases, the tenant has a duty to maintain the property in suitable condition during the lease and surrender it in suitable condition at the end of the lease.

From a contractual standpoint, physicians and healthcare providers who are acquiring commercial property should seek advice and analyze the pros and cons of direct purchase, the various methods of payment (e.g., contract for deed), and leasing options. You should protect yourself with title insurance, and if you are going to take out a mortgage, you certainly need to understand the applicable state laws relating to your rights and responsibilities under such a mortgage to avoid any foreclosure action.

4

Protecting Your Practice and Revenues with CGL (Premises Liability) Insurance

Most healthcare providers have been aware for some time that a malpractice suit can be devastating, both financially and emotionally. Malpractice suits, particularly when there is huge monetary award for the plaintiff, usually make major newspaper headlines and the ten o'clock news on TV. What can be as financially and emotionally draining to a practice and its owners are personal injury suits or other types of lawsuits. These are usually related to something happening to a patient or others on the property of the medical practice. This is when premises liability insurance is extremely important for the owners of a practice.

Unfortunately, a medical practice, like most other businesses, can be liable for injuries or damage on or near its property caused by any of the following:

- A dangerous or defective condition
- Crimes committed on the premise
- Negligent hiring of a dangerous employee

- Pollution
- OSHA (Federal Occupation Safety and Health Act) violations

DANGEROUS OR DEFECTIVE CONDITIONS

Patients and visitors injured by a hidden hazard on the premise of the practice may sue for injuries. This is an example of a dangerous or defective condition. Examples of such hidden hazards include lack of or improperly maintained handrails, defects in steps and landings, accumulations of ice and snow, and inadequate lighting. Usually, the plaintiff in such a case must prove three things to prevail in a lawsuit.

1. An injury must have occurred on the property owned or controlled by the medical practice.
2. The plaintiff must show that the medical practice knew about or should have known about the hazard.
3. The plaintiff must show that the business failed to exercise reasonable care to maintain the premises so that the physical condition of the property does not expose visitors to an unreasonable risk of harm.

Usually the property owner has a continuing duty to inspect the property to discover dangerous conditions and make needed repairs or provide warnings. The responsibility for this ongoing duty to inspect and warn cannot be delegated to others.

CRIMES COMMITTED ON THE PREMISES

In the past, victims of criminal acts such as assault or rape that occurred on a business property usually could not recover from such a business. However, most states now authorize recovery if the victim can prove three things:

1. The victim must show a special relationship with the business/medical practice.
2. The victim must show the business/medical practice failed to take reasonable security measures to protect its patients from attack. Such measures include the

provision/absence of security personnel, procedures, and equipment.

3. The victim must show that reasonable security measures would have prevented the attack.

In some cases, a business/medical practice may also be liable for crimes that occur on nonowned adjacent property, such as parking lots, if the patients of the medical practice use the property and the medical practice encourages its patients to use the nonowned property for its own economic gain.

NEGLIGENT HIRING OF A DANGEROUS EMPLOYEE

Another area becoming particularly relevant in the business world today (with unemployment often being less than 5%) is whether an employer has a duty to investigate for an applicant's criminal record. If the application process "discloses a history of violence," the employer may be liable for subsequent injuries caused by the employee. For example, the medical group may be liable if an employee with a known history of violent crimes rapes a patient. Also, the potential exists for a lawsuit when an employer learns of an employee's unfitness or dangerous habits but fails to take corrective measures such as retraining, reassignment, or discharge.

POLLUTION

Most people today have become well aware of the hazards associated with asbestos. Insurance companies have paid billions of dollars for asbestos and environmental claims. Such large settlements again make headlines with the media. However, in the same way, owners of medical practices and their facilities can be sued for pollution of air or water. Such suits may be for public or private nuisance. Public nuisance requires a reasonable interference with a right that is common to the public. Private nuisance involves an invasion of interest in the private use or enjoyment of land. An example is the need to properly dispose of polluted water in a medical practice. Most medical practices do a good job of taking care of contaminated needles without recognizing the potential for a lawsuit of taking care of contaminated water.

OSHA VIOLATIONS

For years, most hospitals and healthcare providers have been aware of OSHA. OSHA basically governs the health and safety conditions in the workplace. Under OSHA, the federal government has issued numerous occupational health and safety standards that medical practices must comply with, regardless of size. A medical group/practice can be fined for not keeping occupational safety documents required by OSHA. OSHA is enforced against employers through government inspections with notices, citations, fines, and penalties for violations of OSHA standards. Healthcare providers with laboratories and x-ray departments need to understand all of the OSHA regulations but specifically those relating to technical areas such as laboratories and radiology.

CGL INSURANCE

The examples just described are given to help illustrate the broad exposure legally that healthcare providers have when they become owners of a medical practice. A standard commercial general liability (CGL) policy will usually cover most negligent-based premises-liability claims if the damages are for property damage or bodily injury. However, in many cases, claims for emotional distress will not be covered and pollution claims are normally excluded.

It is extremely important to protect yourself in our ever-increasing litigious society. You should consult with your insurance agent/consultant. In addition, you may want to get multiple bids from different insurance companies for your CGL policy because all companies do not cover the same potential hazards. Once you have selected a company for your CGL coverage, it is suggested that you work with them and *develop a prevention program that includes the following ways to help reduce any liability suits and potential loss of revenue:*

- Routinely inspect your property and equipment for all obvious and hidden hazards.
- Correct as many of the identified hazards as you can and place warning signs near any hazards you cannot immediately correct.
- If you are in a high crime area, strongly consider hiring a security guard or service to protect your patients, employees, and equipment.
- Place "employees only" signs on all nonpublic rooms and areas.
- Take extreme cautions in the disposition of contaminated waters, chemicals, and toxic materials.
- Obtain expert assistance on waste storage treatment and disposal, particularly ensuring compliance with OSHA regulations.
- Educate employees, on an ongoing basis, with written documentation that you request them to notify you of any health and safety problems. *Explain to all of your employees your desire for them to help keep the work environment safe.* You may even want to develop a reporting form that employees are asked to complete within one working day of the discovery of any violation of law or observation of unsafe work conditions. Such notice may also be publicly posted throughout the medical facility to ensure that all employees have had the opportunity to become aware of the situation and your request.

Controlling Costs for Improved Revenues through Accurate Cost Accounting

For most of the twentieth century, the traditional accounting for physicians has been on a cost basis. The basic reason for using a cost basis is that most practices have CPAs who do their tax reports, and those CPAs have usually advised them to show all revenue expended as a cost by December 31 of each year so that there would not be "double taxation." That double taxation could occur if, in fact, physicians received revenue that they would pay individual income taxes on and the practice also paid additional taxes on other income not expended by December 31. As practices grow larger and become more sophisticated, and often when practices and groups have grown to the point in their managed care activity where they receive a significant share of their revenue from capitation, different accounting approaches may be suggested by your financial advisors. Such different financial approaches would likely include accrual accounting or activity-based costing. Regardless of the system used, physicians need to understand how their accounting system works, why it was selected, and whether it provides a rational, quantitative system that can help them determine whether their practice is on the right financial track.

COST BEHAVIOR PATTERNS

From a basic accounting standpoint, regardless of the type of cost accounting approach used or suggested by your financial consultant, it is important for physicians to understand certain basics of their costs related to the activity of the practice. Figures 5–1 through 5–4 provide simplistic ways of viewing the following types of costs: fixed, variable, semi-variable, and step-fixed costs.

Without going into great detail, it is fairly obvious from the way the cost line changes on these figures that *there are obvious differences in the way costs can be recognized and described.* The differences primarily relate to the type of "costs" and the type of activity. One of the most common activities is patient volume. For Figure 5–1, assume that the cost referred to is rent for office space. If the practice volume was constant, perhaps totally capitated with 2,000 patients per physician in the practice, the rent for office space would likely be constant.

F I G U R E   5–1

Fixed

Variable

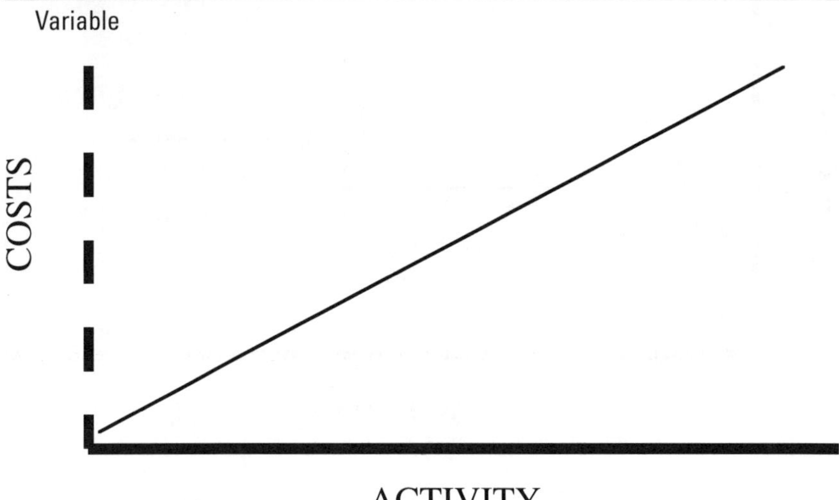

Semi-variable

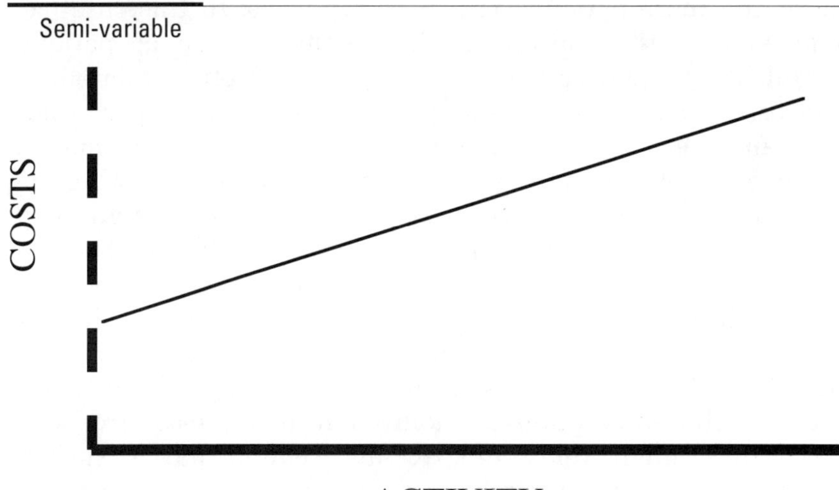

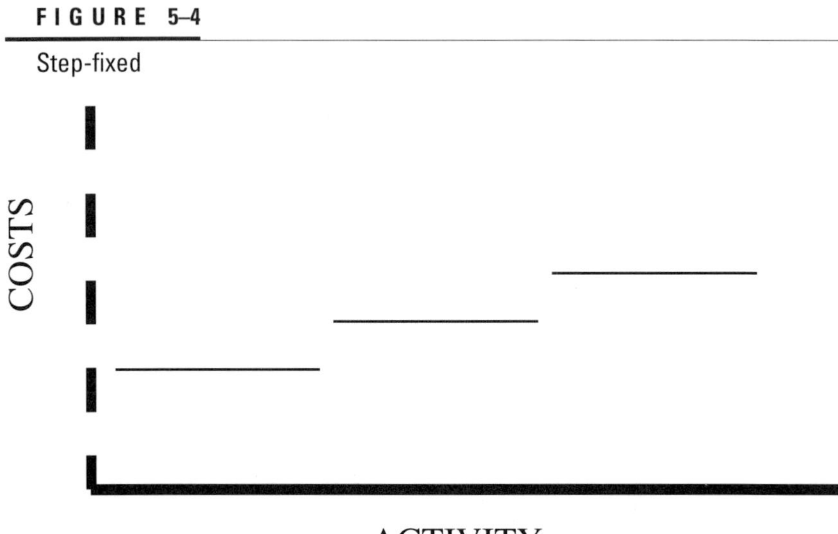

Therefore, a solid horizontal line travels across the chart. This might change dramatically if, in fact, the practice was fee-for-service, in a newly established practice that was attracting more and more patients on a monthly basis. In this case (see Figure 5–2), the continually increasing volume of patients would likely increase the cost of space and other related expenses, such as upkeep, if the practice were to add more space each and every month. In Figure 5–3, some costs are fixed (let's assume that we are now talking about personnel), but when the patient load reaches a certain point, more physicians and support staff are added. These additional costs would then be semivariable costs. In Figure 5–4, a step-fixed type of cost recognition is illustrated. Here, a relatively flat cost is seen for the first thousand patients; then for the next thousand patients, a new additional threshold of costs; and finally with the addition of another thousand patients, additional fixed costs are seen, again these might relate to space and related charges such as maintenance, heat, and light.

The overall approach of indicating these four types of costs is to provide a basic understanding of those areas that you as a physician can control certain expenditures. If you sign a lease for 15,000 square feet, that will be a fixed cost for the term of the lease. However, if you negotiate that lease so that you only pay for the portion of the 15,000 square feet you need on a quarterly basis, your cost then would normally be lower in the first quarter than in the succeeding quarters, assuming that your patient volume continued to increase.

Another basic to be aware of in examining your costs and trying to control them is the distribution of your costs relative to services and nonpatient care support categories. When trying to financially plan for the future and evaluate reimbursement from potential managed care contracts, it is helpful to look at given responsibility centers to determine whether any costs can be controlled in them depending on the types of costs occurring (e.g., fixed versus variable). Examples of various responsibility centers include the following:

- Medicine services by specialty (e.g., family practice, pediatrics, ob-gyn)
- Surgical specialties (e.g., general surgery, orthopedic surgery, thoracic surgery, vascular surgery)
- Ancillary medical services (e.g., laboratory, radiology, optical, physical therapy, speech therapy)
- Medical support services (e.g., appointment scheduling, reception areas, medical records, medical secretaries)
- Occupancy and use (e.g., buildings and grounds, maintenance, housekeeping, security)
- Administrative services (e.g., administration, personnel, employee relations, accounting, management information systems, business office/billing and collections, purchasing/communications, marketing)

Once you have determined what the specific responsibility centers are for your practice, you can then allocate the types of expenditures to each responsibility center as appropriate. For example, you may have the fixed expenses for total occupancy allocated to each of the responsibility centers, depending on the amount of square footage for each responsibility center. Similarly, you may want to approach the distribution of variable expenses, such as supplies, to each of the responsibility centers based on actual use or number of patients seen in a given responsibility area. In such a case, pediatrics would normally have a much higher supply cost than orthopedic surgery, if the variable cost for supplies was based on the number of patient visits divided into the total costs of supplies. It is at this point that you can probably envision a variety of exceptions and variations that depend on the number of specialties in the practices, the number of physicians, the number of capitated patients versus noncapitated patients, the number of actual locations for the total practice, and so on. The point is that there are basic ways to gain a better handle on your total costs/projections than by simply lumping all costs of the practice into one or two major categories after physicians compensation has been removed from total revenue.

The importance of understanding your accounting system is not to make physicians accountants but to determine how physicians can achieve a stronger bottom line. As new payments come into effect from third party payors and as more healthcare services are provided under contract, providers are finding that direct tracking of charges and cost is simply no longer adequate to understand their finances. All forms of overhead must be considered to project cash flows accurately and to develop true costs/profits per contract. The practice dedicated to being financially successful needs to develop a sound financial system that includes not only effective costing systems but a good budget as part of an ongoing business plan. This is not a one time event. This financial information, how it is developed, analyzed, and used for good decision making, is part of an ongoing process.

Many physician groups and partnerships, particularly those that have monthly meetings of partners, engage in some type of planning at their monthly meetings. Often, decisions are made about the capability of certain employees or the necessity to add another physician, but most groups do not do such planning/decision making through a formal budgeting system. In the past, physicians have been able to meet increases in expenses and generate higher personal income through more productivity and higher fees. We are seeing through managed care, and particularly capitation, that there may be a point where fee increases may be eliminated or useless. Additional distributable income must also need to be generated through cost control because revenue will be fixed in a capitated environment. Planning and controlling costs require two dimensions of information: (1) a knowledge of what happens to revenue and costs as activity changes and (2) a knowledge of when cash will be collected and when cash must be paid out. Meaningful cost projections must be based on the amount of resources consumed for the services performed. Physicians and their managers must determine how to accomplish their financial goals within each responsibility/cost center and with each individual's area of responsibility. Cost management information can be a valuable tool to help in making operational decisions. Understanding the behavior of your costs and how to apply cost information properly will give you and your practice managers a significant advantage over competition in managed care environments when negotiating/renegotiating contracts.

Using Financial Planning for Improved Decision Making

Most of us would like to believe that we could do a simple budget each year that would simply state that our projected revenues for the time period would be X, the future expenses would be Y, and the resulting net income would be Z. As medical practices grow, the complexity of the annual budgeting/forecasting process becomes more difficult and certainly more important. The budget itself is the basis for the cost management system of practices. The budget provides a framework for setting priorities, allocating resources, and ultimately monitoring and controlling costs. An effective budget becomes an integral part of management decision making. It must be understood and supported by each physician and practice manager/responsibility center manager.

A major advantage of budgeting is that it requires owners and management personnel to plan in an organized and concentrated way. The process demands that the medical group set aside specific times each year to plan and that these plans reflect how to achieve already-established goals and objectives. Budgeting to be successful also should produce good communication and coordination of the short-range operating plans within the medical group. This becomes more important as the number of responsibility centers grows. Budgeting also helps in the review process for authorization of staff personnel and the use of new additional resources. And last, from an overall standpoint, budgeting can help in the establishment of benchmarks for the evaluation of performance. (Benchmarking is discussed more fully in Chapter 7.) It is essential to have a cost management system and budget in place to establish and use benchmarking through your computer system.

As medical groups grow and the revenues from such groups increase into the millions and tens of millions, simple budgets give way to comprehensive budgets. Many times these comprehensive budget plans will actually consist of several subsections of a total comprehensive budget:

- A profit plan
- A cash budget
- A capital budget
- A projected financial position statement

The comprehensive budget areas require varying degrees of coordination and planning to pull together a series of different parts of the total budgeting process, including the following:

- External financial information that often includes projections of additional patients, potential price increases, use of current and future additional equipment, and influences of other sources such as competition
- The physician's/owner's personal goals and goals for the group, including not only personal income levels but potential change in number of hours available to see patients or changes in the number of patients seen per hour
- Management of resources, including reductions in patient receivables and cost of supplies
- A revenue budget based on varying sources of income from managed care contracts, direct contracts, patient copayments, and fee-for-service activity

- An expense budget broken down by the various categories discussed earlier (i.e., fixed, variable, semi-variable, or step-fixed based on activity changes)
- Net cash flow revenues, which are extremely important to project and follow to ensure proper bank balances to pay large cost items such as malpractice insurance premiums, and additional revenue/cost from planned major activities such as the acquisition of another physician's practice or the sale of certain equipment
- Projected cash balances at any one point in time available for either investing or borrowing as opposed to financing capital acquisitions

All of these will probably be much clearer when you do your financial planning based on activity forecasts. Four basic elements should be considered when determining future fiscal activity: historical trends of patient services, physician and support staff volumes, internal factors such as increased hours of operations, and external factors such as reduced Medicare reimbursement.

USING YOUR BUDGET ACTIVITY TO CONTROL COSTS

Although developing and using a budget can initially be time-consuming, it is well worth the time expended because it will provide a sound approach for physicians and their practice managers to manage their cost and planning activities to meet financial objectives. Just as there are various ways that costs can be defined (e.g., average cost, historical costs), there are different ways of budgeting.

In the rest of the 1990s and the years of the new century ahead, there will likely be continued change in the healthcare delivery "business." With continual change, most physician practices may benefit from developing a flexible budget because when there is constant change, it is often difficult to estimate future activity volumes and the cost related to those volume changes. A flexible budget will accommodate changes in numbers and types of patients, patient encounters, and activity volume for those encounters such as lab and x-ray. From a planning approach, a flexible budget enables management to analyze cost on the basis of a series of individual volume forecasts coupled with estimates of fixed and variable costs for each type of activity. When developing a flexible budget, it is important to develop corresponding performance reports that allow periodic (quarterly, semi-annually, or annually) evaluation of how well the practice is meeting its budgeted projection. Budgets should be used as an ongoing management tool for the practice because flexible budgets help physicians and their practice managers with the key issue of budget variances. With a flexible budget, when variances occur and are observed in the quarterly evaluations, the budget can be relatively easily adjusted to reflect actual activity levels. When this happens, the data become much more meaningful and decision making on how to respond to issues such as "lower revenue" can be much more specific. This chapter is not designed to provide great detail on this topic or to teach cost accounting. However, it is important to understand that tools and techniques are available in the accounting arena that can be of significant value to physicians in the United States today, where healthcare is truly becoming a business.

There are some basic guidelines for developing a flexible budget and cost management system. These can be relatively simple, or depending on the given group practice and its activities, they can be time-consuming. However, it is important to create a framework from which the decision makers in the practice can then use the data effectively. As an overall approach to developing a flexible budget and a cost management system, physicians and their practice managers will need to do the following:

- Identify responsibility centers.
- Apply revenues and cost to each separate responsibility center.
- Allocate costs of support service departments in a fair and equitable manner to the revenue-producing responsibility centers.
- Calculate the cost of each procedure or service.
- Determine the overall costs for the services provided in each of the practice's facilities.

Without going into great detail on budgeting, particularly because the goal is not to make you an accountant or financial manager (and because it is assumed that you don't want to be either), it is sufficient to say that this chapter has given the basis for developing a total accounting system for your medical practice. As your financial management system is developed, it needs to be developed and coordinated with your computer system. Once that happens, the real dividends of the time and effort that you spend on this activity start to pay off. Two examples of these payoffs are measuring physician productivity and being able to analyze the financial impact of capitated contracts.

Let's take a brief look at these two examples. Over the last few years, particularly with the growth of managed care, measuring physician productivity has become an extremely important part of the "business" side of healthcare delivery. Much has been written about it and much has been said about it, not all of it very flattering. However, it has gotten to the point of often being considered standard operating procedure. Some physician productivity measurement activity can be as simple and straightforward as total gross revenue generated by a particular physician; certainly in the days when most medical practices received fee-for-service reimbursement, this was considered fairly normal. However, today as physicians are moving more and more into group practices, multiple specialty practices, and integrated physician network practices, there becomes a tendency to tie physician productivity into income distribution systems. When this is done, most groups try to approach their income distribution system activity by looking at not only revenue generated but cost-effectiveness of that revenue. To approach it in this manner, the medical practice needs to have a good financial practice system. Typically, the financial management system should be able to compare actual production and cost activities with budgeted projections and then make comparisons with the total group and/or other physicians of the same specialty practices in similar medical service areas. For some specialties, and in particular for larger groups with a greater share of managed care patients, the physician productivity measurement will often include comparisons of productivity by looking at procedural complexity and case intensity. This gets us into the whole issue of a Resource Based Relative Value System (RBRVS). Again, when it becomes important to look at RBRVS, it is important to have a comprehensive financial management system.

Similar to the last example, the financial management system is almost a necessity for those groups and physicians accepting capitated reimbursement. With capitation, it must be remembered that there is an important difference between fixed costs and variable costs. The importance here goes back to the basis for having a viable financial practice under capitation (i.e., revenue is fixed under capitation, and as costs go up from additional patient visits and services, the opportunity for net revenue in the practice decreases). Therefore, it is at this point that determination of fixed versus variable cost becomes very important to planning for the practice over a projected period (twelve months or more). Usually, the fixed costs in a practice are not capable of being reduced except on an annual basis. Should the need arise for reducing cost on an intermediate basis, the identification of the variable costs then play a significant role in helping identify how the practice can be more cost-effective, particularly assuming that revenue is going to stay constant under a capitated contract. A good example of this is employees. There will always be a need for a core group of employees for support staff. The time to take a look at potential variable costs is when the activity levels change based on one of our performance measurements (i.e., patient visits). If temps are hired to provide support when patient volume rises, these temporary employees can be let go and the variable cost for that additional support goes away when it is no longer needed (e.g., when patient volume decreases). Whether it is temporary employees, supplies, maintenance activities, or equipment leasing, all variable expenses, and some fixed expenses that might be changed in the future into variable expenses, need to be considered from the financial planning standpoint. Adjusting the ratio of fixed and variable cost within a medical practice is a part of dealing with the business changes that come with managed care reimbursement, and particularly capitation. *Like most other businesses today, health-care must be approached from the standpoint that change is inevitable and that the successful practice will plan ahead to be prepared for such inevitable changes.* The accounting and financial management systems for practices go hand in hand with the computer software and hardware to provide physicians and their staff the capability to not only plan ahead but be successful in that planning.

Compensation Planning to Achieve Financial Goals: Dividing Practice Income with Partners and Associates

Most physicians in solo practice have little need to be concerned about compensation planning, particularly through income distribution systems, because by and large what they receive is what is left after paying the bills of the practice. However, as more and more physicians join together in either single specialty practices, multiple specialty group practices, physician networks, physician hospital organizations (PHOs), or clinics without walls, the need for compensation planning becomes particularly important. This is especially true because all physicians in one practice are basically used to one system; when they move organizationally to a different format (e.g., single specialty to multiple specialty group practice), the likelihood is that the income distribution system will change. This change may be good or bad, or perceived as good or bad. But because most physicians are particularly sensitive to any potential decreases in their income, income distribution planning needs to be approached carefully, particularly if the result of such planning might be a new income distribution system where some physicians might make more money than others.

Let's put this discussion into perspective: With the increases in group practices in the United States over the last twenty-five years, the changes in income distribution systems have created a general shift toward the following four types of compensation systems:

1. Production
2. Salary plus incentives
3. Straight salary
4. Salary and production

In addition to these four basic types of compensation plans, for those groups that have something other than straight salary, each group will more than likely have its adaptation of one of the other three primary types of plans. Even if straight salaries are the general type of compensation for a group, there are often other differences relating to economic factors such as pension plans, car allowances, educational trips, and vacation that may make a significant difference in total compensation between two groups both on straight salary compensation plans. Basically, advice for physicians and medical groups wanting to study, change, or create a new compensation system is that if you have seen one income distribution system, you have seen one income distribution system. The reason for making such a statement is that income distribution systems should be specifically designed for the physicians of a given medical practice in a specific location.

Given the uniqueness of the income distribution system and its relationship to the providers themselves as well as their environment, certain key things need to be considered when determining appropriate physician compensation for a given medical practice.

THE MARKETPLACE

The compensation in New York City is likely to be considerably different than that in a small town in a rural state like South Dakota. Other marketplace components that are becoming increasingly important are the number of similar specialists in the same medical service area as well as other competing medical groups that may be reached via good roads up to an hour or more away.

MANAGED CARE

The growth and impact of managed care in a specific medical service area will greatly influence the type of compensation system being designed for a specific medical practice (i.e., this becomes particularly important with the growth of capitated reimbursement from managed care companies).

FRINGE BENEFITS

In certain medical service areas, the physicians in a practice may believe that it is desirable to reduce actual salary paid monthly and in turn spend more money on fringe benefits, including vacations. Some physicians would rather have an extra two weeks vacation than another $20,000. Sometimes, the location of the practice might encourage the use of more vacation time and therefore less revenue being generated by the physicians for income distribution.

PRACTICE PHILOSOPHY

Some medical practices believe that they are in an environment in which they must be available to see patients nights and weekends, whereas other practices maintain fairly regular hours from 8 to 5, Monday through Friday. Given the differences in the marketplace, practices that feel the need to be competitively open at least six days a week often find their compensation planning and results significantly different from the practice that is open only from 8 to 5, Monday through Friday. Obviously other significant decisions need to be made when a hospital is involved in the patient care activities of the physicians in the group. When some physicians spend a significant portion of their time in one hospital (e.g., a cardiologist performing cardiac catheterization), the income distribution formula may need to be adjusted if that practice has merged with another cardiology group whose cardiac catheterization cardiologist goes to multiple hospitals, including some an hour or more away.

QUALITY OF SERVICE ACTIVITIES

Peer Reviews

As many practices grow from one to two or even two to three physicians, most such groups find that all of the physicians are aware of each others' practice styles and outcomes. However, as groups get larger and have multiple locations of their practices, the use of peer review activities creates an opportunity to include certain standards, depending on the medical specialty(ies), that can be used as part of physician compensation planning.

Patient Satisfaction Surveys

In the urban marketplace, especially where the competition for patients increases the need to use marketing techniques, we often see the results of patient satisfaction surveys in ads. Although this is true of some medical groups, particularly groups in which the competition is also using patient satisfaction surveys, the results of such surveys can also be used as part of a physician compensation formula.

Outcomes Studies

Most healthcare providers have been hearing about outcomes studies for some years. Often, they make for interesting journal reading. However, today we find that the results of outcomes studies are now being used, much like patient satisfactory surveys, for marketing purposes. This is particularly true in areas where there is strong managed care competition between competing HMOs and PPOs. Again, where the inclusion or exclusion of individual physicians or medical practices from managed care panels can be the result of outcomes studies, it may be beneficial to include such outcomes studies as part of physician compensation planning/systems.

PRODUCTION

Dollars Billed

In the more traditional fee-for-service environment of the 50s, 60s, and 70s, we would have seen dollars billed as the major factor involved with a physician's production. As such, in those groups that were developing production-only compensation systems, this particular component was the key variable.

Dollars Collected

In the 1970s, with the federal government encouraging the growth of HMOs and reimbursement starting to be decreased, dollars collected became a new factor that was often a more critical part of physician compensation systems.

Patient Visits

Depending on the medical specialty, the number of patient visits has also been a key component in physician compensation planning. This was traditionally important for the fee-for-service environment, but as managed care grew, this also became an important part of compensation planning particularly for capitated reimbursement.

RBRVUs

For practices that have spent considerable time trying to cope with decreasing reimbursement and changes in reimbursement formulas from Medicare, an understanding of the RBRVU factors has become very important in income distribution planning and actual compensation itself.

COST-EFFECTIVENESS

Resource Consumption

In a managed care marketplace where traditional reimbursement has gone down instead of up, for medical practices to maintain their net revenues, it is important for the practice to be as cost-effective as possible. In the good old days when the cost of employees and supplies could have been offset by patient fee increases, there was not as strong a concern about being cost-effective, particularly through resource consumption. Today, as supplies become more and more expensive, to say nothing of the cost of support personnel, the physicians who work toward the best resource consumption approach while still producing quality care outcomes will usually be considered the most cost-effective providers. This typically has created a need for a new approach to income planning (i.e., no longer are all costs always shared equally, but now with new accounting and computer systems, costs can be allocated to various cost centers on a consumption basis). These cost centers can be as small as one provider.

Control of Unnecessary Use

Again, as managed care has grown in a given medical service area, usually the managed care companies through case management or other means, have tried to control unnecessary use, particularly hospital use. This philosophy has carried over to medical groups, particularly medical groups that are capitated for all or part of their patient care revenue. In these situations, the physician compensation planning usually should consider how to reward the physicians who do an appropriate job of controlling unnecessary use, notably that use is going to be a major cost to the medical practice.

THE INCOME DISTRIBUTION PLANNING PROCESS

Understanding Individual Providers' Needs

As healthcare providers join the system today, they have a need for income that is different than the providers who may have joined the system thirty years ago. Today, physicians completing their residency often have incurred loans of up to or more than $100,000. In addition to the individual needs of the members of a group practice, group financial objectives also need to be met through the course of the group's revenue generation activity. Therefore, learning as much as possible up front about the following areas, for both physicians individually and the practice, is desirable:

- Individual financial needs and long-range financial goals
- Support of the total practice as well as various specialties if more than one specialty is involved with the medical practice
- Financial objectives for the group, including growth and capital needs
- Recognition of changes in the managed care and Medicare reimbursement programs
- Financial needs to recognize and provide for retirement of older physicians
- Flexibility planning for changes in individuals' financial needs (e.g., children going to college)
- Recognition of changes in patient mix and resulting revenues
- Determination of how individuals and the group will react to and accommodate any major change in their compensation
- Recognition of current major fringe benefits that can be considered part of compensation

Before deciding how to use the answers to these questions, it is important to recognize that an income distribution system should not be considered as a separate entity from the rest of the organization's total planning and activity. *Specifically planning for income distribution changes should normally follow planning for the short- and long-range goals of the practice itself.*

What are those factors that the group may want to achieve via their planning and income distribution system? Various factors logically included in such strategic compensation planning include the following:

- Economies of scale through sharing of resources
- Recognition of competition in the marketplace
- Analysis of the financial impact of managed care growth on the practice

- Professional and personal goals
- Maintenance of compatibility among professionals and staff within the practice
- Determination of necessary changes in practice patterns, services, and locations
- Development of a mission statement or adherence to a current mission statement that focuses on quality of care and patient outcomes

Much has been written about strategic planning. In today's environment, it is important that total strategic planning be done yearly, particularly in markets that are rapidly changing. As the strategic planning process is finalized, planning for an income distribution system can start as part of the activity necessary to help meet the objectives of the strategic planning process.

Typical Goals for Income Distribution Systems

In part to meet the objectives for both the income distribution system and the strategic planning process, it is important to have a good medical income distribution system that includes the following characteristics:

- A system that provides appropriate income for every physician and provider
- A system that is easy to understand
- A system that rewards "good" performance
- A system that results in a fair and consistent distribution

A good income distribution system is a work in process. It should be flexible in design so that it will change as the needs of the group and individuals change. To be effective, the income distribution system must recognize differences in various physicians' work, specialty, effort, and contributions to the medical practice. From a philosophical standpoint, income distribution systems should reward and not penalize. Just like the strategic planning process, the income distribution planning process should be flexible enough so that it can be changed, and if not changed, at least reviewed annually to ensure that it is meeting the objectives talked about earlier in this chapter. Table 7–1 gives a general overview of how different types of compensation systems help meet some of the objectives talked about earlier (i.e., cost-effectiveness/budget control, use management and quality of care outcomes, recognize that specific plans can target one or more areas changing the results).

Results of income distribution systems vary based on the key goals of the medical practice. For example, many groups have concerns regarding budget/financial control, use controls, and quality controls. Various systems have different results when gauged by the planning objectives. As an example, a capitation system usually has good results for the first two goals but can produce poor results in the quality control arena.

PLANNING COMPONENTS FOR NEW SYSTEMS

There is "no one best" system of income distribution for all medical groups. Therefore, when you develop a new income distribution system, use the planning process components just described while working through the following major components:

- Start with a goal of determining a fair and equitable income distribution system for all members of the group.
- Specifically, determine what is happening in your given medical service area, particularly as far as the future can be anticipated for reimbursement changes from managed care and Medicare.

TABLE 7–1

Typical physician compensation planning goals and how they are usually met by different types of compensation systems

Type of Compensation	Budget Control	Use	Quality
Fee-for-service	Poor	Poor	Good
Salary	Good	Fair	Good
Capitation	Good	Good	Poor
Salary plus incentives	Good	Good	Good

- Recognize which fringe benefits and quality of life issues are most important to the physicians in the medical practice.

- Recognize which factors create unusual expenses for the medical practice.

- Determine the best way to recognize and reward the work effort/production of physicians. Such work effort/production can be quantified in various ways, including dollars billed, dollars collected, patient visits, and RBRVUs.

- Realize that cost-effectiveness will become increasingly important as the medical practice increases its managed care activity. Prepare for the future by looking at clinical outcomes. Managed care companies often do their own outcomes studies and patient satisfaction surveys. Therefore, medical groups should do their own studies internally to help strengthen marketing to third party payors, as well as to possibly use the studies as part of their income distribution system.

- Recognize nonpatient care components in determining physician compensation and value to the group. Such components include administrative activities such as being a managing partner, teaching, marketing, developing referral physician relationships, and contributing time and effort to local organizations.

As you go through the process and develop a template for an income distribution system/change to your current system, the following are recommendations to help in the implementation of your recommendation.

- Base your compensation planning on the medical group's history, culture, needs, and practice standards.

- Gain physician support for the process by getting/asking for objective participation and input into goals, problems, and recommendations for change.

- All discussions of new compensation plans/changes should be put into the context of the medical practice's philosophy, total goals, and objectives. Determine which changes will require physician support to be successfully implemented and determine how that support from the various members of the medical staff can be achieved.

+ Determine strategies that will be necessary to resolve key issues and implementation in the future.

+ Develop an implementation plan that includes education for all participants and a process for gaining consensus among them.

Figure 7–1 may be particularly helpful for groups who are moving more into managed care/capitation reimbursement. It is an example of an income distribution system for a group of ten physicians in a single specialty group and is designed for flexibility and accommodations to individual and group dynamics. It is also based on a given medical service area and a recognition that a growing percentage of revenue for the medical group was being generated from managed care contracts. This specific example was developed by John McCally with two former colleagues, Ms. Madeline Miskowic, now President of Challenge Health Network in Pompano Beach, Florida and Jonathan Lewis, now a partner in a healthcare consulting and accounting firm in San Diego, California.

FIGURE 7–1

Key Components of Model Physician Compensation System for a Single Specialty Practice

A group of ten physicians, a single specialty group, an example of one of those physicians who has been with the group for nine years.

Distributable Income for Physician Compensation (DIPC), estimated after paying expenses: $2,000,000.

1. Base Salary = 25%
   ($2,000,000 × 25%) = $500,000

   Dr. "X" = $500,000 divided by 10 = $50,000

2. Seniority Factor = 5% of DIPC
   Seniority Split (5% × $2,000,000) = $100,000
   Seniority calculated by internal point system based on number of years service.

   Dr. "X" 9/140 points × $100,000 = $6,428.57.
   *(Note: 140 is the total number of seniority years for all ten physicians.)

continued

F I G U R E   7–1—Cont'd

3. "Production Credits" = 50%
 ($2,000,000 × 50%) = $1,000,000
 Dr. "X"'s Production Credits:
 (Maximum allowable is 2 points of each 5 production categories or 10% of
  total points for this pool.)

Cost per Patient	1.5
Credit	
Utilization Credit	1.0
Fee-for-Service Equivalent Credit (>35 patients per day)	1.0
Patient Service Credit	0
Case Management Credit	1.5

> **Dr "X"'s Total Product Credits = 5 points = 0.083% of total
> production credits × $1,000,000 = $83,000**

*(Total points available for all doctors was 60 points.)

4. "Performance" credits = 15%
 ($2,000,000 × 15%) = $300,000
 (Maximum allowable is 2 points for each of the 5 performance categories
  or 10% of total points for this pool.)

Continuing Education Credit	1.0
Board Certified through Two Boards	1.0
General Contributions to Group	1.5
Administrative Duties to Group	0.5
Overall Performance Contribution	1.5

> **Dr. "X"'s Total Performance Credits = 5.5 points = 9.2% of total
> performance credits × $300,000 = $27,500**

*(Total points available for all doctors was 60 points.)

5. "At Risk" withhold for extra costs/possible bonuses = 5%
 Money held back this accounting period (usually calendar year) for next
  year: 5% × $2,000,000 = $100,000
 Funds for distribution from last accounting period: $50,000 includes
  interest earned.
 As approved by the Board of Directors:
  Equal split for good team cost effectiveness in:
   –Patient Encounters
   –Appropriate Number of Referrals
   –Appropriate Amount of Lab, X-Ray, and Treatment

> **Dr. "X"'s Bonus Income = $50,000 divided by 10 physicians = $5,000**

> **Breakdown of Dr. "X"'s TOTAL INCOME DISTRIBUTION:**

–Base Salary	$50,000.00
–Seniority	$ 6,428.57
–Production	$83,000.00
–Performance	$27,500.00
–Bonus	$ 5,000.00

> **Dr. "X"'s TOTAL INCOME is $171,928.57**

Figure 7–1 variables:

1. *Base salary:* Up to 25% of each physician's total compensation may be based on his or her medical specialty, taking into consideration competitive national, state, and even regional compensation norms. Fringe benefit allowances may be considered (e.g., the amount of benefit expenses to be paid by the group each month for each physician).

2. *Seniority:* Up to 5% of total dollars available for distribution may be allocated using points for each year of tenure.

3. *"Production" credits:* Up to 50% may include a cost per patient (CPP) credit. This is done through comparative analysis of CPP within the practice or within the community.
   - Utilization credits may be considered for capitated income. This generally refers to a physician's referral pattern within and outside the group.
   - Some groups may use a fee-for-service equivalent credit, which can prevent penalizing the physician who has high volume and difficult case loads.
   - Another "production" credit may be a patient service credit. This comes in the form of actual quality assurance/patient service surveys. Some clinics have such survey questionnaires that patients fill out when they leave.
   - Another credit that can be given is case management credit. This credit is given for good case management from start to finish. This type of credit is likely to be common in the future under managed care and mandatory outcomes data reporting requirements.

4. *Performance incentives:* These can be weighted up to 15%. They are used as a tool to motivate, evaluate, and commend a physician's contribution to the practice/group. Examples of these credits are continuing medical education credit, board certification credit, and general contributions to the group (e.g., updating and improving medical or operational procedures within the group). Finally, there can be

administrative contribution credit for those who take on delegated spokesman duties or medical operational duties (e.g., medical director).

5. *"At risk" compensation:* This can be up to 5% of the total available income pool, withheld from distribution for at least one accounting period (one year) and given as bonuses when group objectives have been attained. Group objectives may include patient encounter targets met, number of referral targets met, appropriate use of the number of lab and x-ray tests performed, and overall financial objectives being met.

As mentioned, Figure 7–1 creates a hypothetical model designed for flexibility. Obviously, whether five physicians, ten physicians, or more were in the group, the figures would change but the flexibility in the model is something that can be used by most groups contemplating change in their income distribution system based on increases in managed care/capitated reimbursement.

This flexible formula provides a rational and equitable approach to distributing income, including dollars from managed care/capitated income. However, because every medical group is unique in its makeup of physicians, specialty distributions, patient volumes, managed care contracts, and financial goals/growth, a new income distribution system is recommended for each individual group going through this process. Recognizing that there is no one right income distribution system, the process in this chapter may be used as an outline in the planning and development of first your goals and objectives, then the plan, and finally, the implementation of that plan.

8

CHAPTER

Select and Use the Right Computer to Improve Your Financial Activity and Management Control

The age of the computer, as the primary tool in multiple aspects of healthcare, is not going to arrive in the twenty-first century; it's here now. Many physicians are beginning to understand this. The computer is commonly used today as an aid in the diagnosis of patient's problems; it is used from the most sophisticated level, such as an MRI, to a more routine level, such as the processing of commonly ordered laboratory tests. In many environments, the computer is used to communicate the results of patients' test and examinations from one location to another. The clinical examples could go on for many pages, but the key point is that the computer is also equally important for physicians today in terms of having successful financial practice management activity. The fact that there are more than four hundred different medical software packages available today should help bring this issue into focus for all physicians, regardless of where they practice and in what type of practice arrangement. The hardware and software for a physician's medical practice goes far beyond the computerized billing systems that were prevalent fifteen to twenty years ago. PCs have became faster and more reasonably priced, so physician practices don't need larger mainframe arrangements. This has rapidly pushed the changes for physician uses.

The ongoing revolution in hardware size and speed, coupled with the reduction in cost of new hardware, has been a blessing and a problem for many physicians and their practice managers. The good news is that the speed of computers and their size have been constantly improving. The bad news is that the total cost for multiple computerized services/activities has similarly been expanding, as has the cost of all others aspects of medical practice. To coincide with the increased capability and speed of computers for physician offices, and their interface with hospitals when appropriate, there has been a tremendous surge in companies developing appropriate helpful software for physicians and their offices to take them beyond the original business technology. An example of this is software to help move physicians from the old "peg board" type of billing system to ongoing cash management collection programs.

The changes in the software packages for physicians and their practices will no doubt continue to change annually. Many of the software companies have R&D departments and programmers devoted to developing the next level of new activity and service, which can help create better financial control and better integration of total patient activity. Some of this integration activity is already being seen with electronic medical records being part of the new software available today.

The rush of the managed care train down the one-way track toward total care via contracts has probably provided the greatest demand for greater change to the medical practice software programs of the past. Particularly in the larger, urban areas where managed care has penetrated more than 50% of the marketplace, physician practices are almost completely reliant on their computer system to ensure proper billing and reimbursement to and through a multitude of HMOs and PPOs. This is extremely important as more and more capitation contracts become part of the managed care reimbursement scene in any given medical service area. In addition to managed care, we now have Medicare basically requiring "clean" claims to be submitted electronically. For those practices serving the Medicare population, the new requirement for Medicare means having a computer system capable of meeting their requirements. This is important for physicians and their practice managers because the type of information and correct claim submissions to HCFA can now provide practices with the ability to know whether their reimbursement is correct or why they are not getting any reimbursement when their claims are rejected by Medicare carriers.

As mentioned elsewhere in this book, many physicians over the last ten years have moved from solo practices into group practices and from group practices into multiple specialty practices, often for the purpose of economy of scale. This is particularly important when it comes to the purchase and use of improved computer systems. In addition, because it is important for physician practices to have the capability to negotiate appropriate managed care contracts and then be able to track those contract reimbursements, the new computer packages and hardware are designed to help physicians achieve their goals in this area.

We already know that every medical service area will be different from the standpoint of managed care penetration and Medicare population, so there will be differences from one practice to the next as to what they need in their software. In our consulting activity with various physician practices and medical groups across the country, we have developed a rational approach to selecting new software. The first section of this approach is to determine what is needed today. The second part in the planning for new software is what will be needed in the next one to three years in the particular medical service area for the medical practice to remain competitive and control their finances (see Figures 8–1 and 8–2).

Figures 8–1 and 8–2 are meant to provide a starting place for any given medical practice considering upgrading into an improved hardware/software system. Frankly, both of these figures also should include additional categories specific to a practice, depending on the individual practice growth pattern and medical service area, as well as the type of clinical practice and hospital arrangements for the physicians and their patients. Additional, individual practices need to look ahead to the types of new services planned for the future, and whether the

Typical Software Needs for Today's Medical Practice Software

* Patient medical information
* Patient reminder system
* Appointment scheduling
* Patient billing
* HMO verification of enrollees/patients
* Insurance coordination/direct on-line submission of claims
* HMO/PPO reporting/submission
* Receivables management/collection program
* Collections tracking by patient class and HMO/PPO/insurance company
* Medicare clean claims submission and review
* CPT/ICD-9 coding cross-reference
* Refund check processing
* Patient receipt payment processing

Optional Software Services That Are Likely To Be Needed in the Next One to Three Years

* Capitation tracking
* Incurred but not reported (IBNR) expense tracking
* Patient status tracking
* Drug use
* EMR (electronic medical record) interface
* Patient chart tracking
* Management exception reporting
* Multiple site cost/revenue reporting

practice is likely to become part of a larger integrated practice activity, such as a single specialty medical network. The answers to these future activity decisions may require new computer software.

NEXT STEPS TO AN IMPROVED COMPUTER SYSTEM: AN RFP

As mentioned at the start of this chapter, there are literally hundreds of vendors who all have the "latest, best, and cheapest" system available. Because most physicians and their practice managers/administrators have many other things to worry about than who is the newest or best computer company, it is important to follow what is a fairly standard procedure in other industries; that is, a request for proposal (RFP) should be developed and sent to various local, regional, and in some cases, national hardware/software vendors. Physicians and their practice managers may want to get assistance in developing requests for proposals from their accountants or practice consultants. *If they do not develop a standardized request for proposal, there is no way to make appropriate comparisons between products and companies when multiple vendors submit their proposals to the physicians and practice managers.* The request for a proposal should start with getting input from all members of the physician's organization as to what's working today and what isn't working. Someone should be assigned to develop a list of what areas need to be looked at in the future, specifically what can be improved electronically (you may want to give your staff copies of Figures 8–1 and 8–2).

Again, with so many vendors in the field today, most practices will want to limit their responses to RFPs to a manageable number, which is probably ten or less. A good way to determine which ten to send your RFP to would be to attend a national meeting of the Medical Group Management Association (MGMA), where numerous healthcare hardware/software vendors exhibit. Another way is to talk to other practices that are of comparable size and specialty in your medical service area or a similar service area elsewhere. As part of the RFP that you develop for sending to various vendors, it is important to provide them with several key bits of information:

- The size of your practice currently
- The amount and growth trends of patient and financial activity on a monthly and annual basis
- The projections for growth in the above areas
- Whether you have established a budget for this expense of new hardware/software
- How much assistance you need/want from a vendor in making the computer conversion and training for/implementing a new system

EVALUATING THE RESPONSES TO YOUR RFP

If you have adequately assessed your needs, both current and future, and developed an appropriate RFP, the responses to your RFP should be relatively consistent in format, which will make the evaluation of responses to your RFP relatively painless. Again, this is a time when you may want to use a professional consultant or your accounting firm to assist you in grading and evaluating the responses you have received. If, in fact, you receive ten responses, it is recommended that you grade them on a scale of one to ten, and after grading them, select the top three to come to your practice and make a personal presentation to those who would be using/making a decision on a new system. Besides cost, it is suggested that you focus on whether the proposing vendor has had experience with your type of practice, is knowledgeable about your location, and whether the vendor has trained and capable people available locally to install the system, train your employees, and provide ongoing technical support. It is also important that before the purchase decision is made, the final hardware/software vendors should be asked to try to determine how their hardware/software can make your practice more efficient and help create a better bottom line, as opposed to simply being a cost of doing business.

Using Your New Computer System for Increased Contracting and Better Reimbursement

There is no doubt that as the number of HMOs and PPOs continues to grow (currently approaching 1,700, to say nothing of the direct contracting with employers and business coalitions), the need for increased data is growing daily. As a provider, you will be constantly asked for new and more information as the third party payors become more sophisticated in how they use healthcare data. In many cases, third party payors will request specific information and capabilities, including the ability to do the following:

- Demonstrate services, values, and patient satisfaction through outcomes measurement data and surveys
- Control the cost of care provided to specific plan enrollees
- Manage financial risk through capitation or other risk-based reimbursement structures

Medical practices that can satisfy all of these needs can often find competitive advantages in their given marketplace.

One way practices can gain an edge in contracting with payors is to provide effective outcomes reporting.

MAKING YOUR COMPUTER INFORMATION WORK FOR YOUR PRACTICE

Various types of outcomes reporting are relevant to managed care positioning, including clinical outcomes, economic outcomes, and subjective patient perceptions and functional status. This is particularly true as more surgery is done in ambulatory surgical centers and more procedures and more elaborate laboratory tests are done on an outpatient basis, often in a medical group's office. The items that many of the payors are looking for often involve individual or episodic types of services; in other cases, outcomes may be longitudinal and based on long-term services and outcomes for a patient or for patient groups.

Economic outcomes are based on the cost of care, often expressed as a cost for each procedure. These outcomes are often essential for determining appropriate reimbursement, and they usually form the basis for contract renegotiations. Outcomes based on patient perception and functional status include service timelines, convenience, perceived effectiveness, and the extent to which such care meets patient expectations. Such outcomes can also influence contract negotiations and, much more important, the reimbursement levels.

Outcomes measures usually achieve optimal effectiveness when coupled with appropriate benchmarks. These benchmarks, using comparative data from practice organizations such as the Medical Group Management Association (MGMA), provide objective assessment of your practice relevant to your peers. Benchmarking for quality care improvement is often seen when protocols and practice guidelines have been developed and implemented. As benchmarking becomes mandated by payors in the marketplace (as is the case in some marketplaces now, and will undoubtedly be mandated in more marketplaces in the future), the tools for quality improvement will often be coupled with the benchmarking that practices do. At this point, your management information system and computer hardware will need to be capable of flexibility and redesigned growth.

The MGMA is taking benchmarking to the next level. They have been benchmarking on productivity and efficiency and through their activity have identified "better practice" guidelines that can be adopted by other groups in comparable benchmarking studies. It is at this point that we now can see that benchmarking that is used to compare numbers has now gone to a new dimension; that is, improving the process of care. Such improvement is what needs to be measured in your outcomes activity by your computer system and then used when marketing and renegotiating your managed care contracts.

Providers no doubt will continue to increase their output of information because the payors will continue to increase their demand for information. The key is to recognize that providers must be able to report appropriate information and must use that information in the most advantageous way possible. Much of the data will come from your outcomes-based information activity. Although outcomes criteria may vary among third party payors, some fairly basic standards are likely to be common to all payors, including the following:

- Care must be appropriate. It must be the correct care for the patient, provided at the right time, and supported by current medical standards of care.
- Care must be performed well. It must represent standards of care and be rendered with the necessary level of appropriate provider skill and resources to optimize success.
- Care must achieve anticipated results that lead to improved health or function for the patient.

WHAT INFORMATION IS IMPORTANT TO BENCHMARK

To determine what type of information would be best for you to benchmark, it is important to know who your patients are and what your payor mix is. Using this information as a base, you may want to determine whether you will select different types of benchmarks for the different types of patients (e.g., Medicare patients, HMO patients, fee-for-service patients). As mentioned earlier, productivity benchmarks with other physicians in the same specialty may be helpful for internal and external evaluation. However, in some cases, your own practice activity may be the most important benchmark possible, particularly if you are going to use performance data to help you negotiate contracts locally. In such a case, one method of starting your analysis for benchmarking criteria would be to develop a listing of how you provide care and service for different types of patients in your practice. This listing might start like a flowchart from the types of services provided by all office personnel when the patient calls for an appointment and all other services and activities that are done before and during a patient's visit, including the physician services. Whether the practice is single specialty or multiple specialty, if such a charting of the clinical issues is done for all physicians of the same specialty, the result will be the start of recognizing the differences in practice patterns among partners and the development of agreed-on clinical pathways. The development of clinical pathways and benchmarks and the monitoring of those benchmarks through the use of your computer system will often reduce total costs of your group practice, particularly when benchmarking is combined with cost analysis for various segments of patient care.

Collecting and analyzing outcomes data can be time-consuming. However, there will hopefully be certain activities that can save time for physicians in the process. Such activities might include using the F-36 Health Status Questionnaire so that physicians have an idea of what trouble areas to look for before they actually see the patient. Electronic aids such as scanners and touch-screen computers for data entry are actually speeding up the total process considerably and often eliminating doctors from having to hand write repetitive information. If we accept as a given that third party payors and government entities are going to require information, then we can easily visualize using our systems to save a great deal of time for physicians and staff, as opposed to creating reports from scratch. It is also safe to say that using your computer system will not only be faster but also often much more accurate. If you also accept the premise that collecting information and putting it into reports is a standard in the healthcare business activity today, and is going to become even larger in the future, then we all can basically understand that there will be more basic cost involved in doing this activity, whether manually or with your computer system. It costs money either way, and it is going to cost less if the practice plans on how to do it efficiently and productively, which usually means using your computer systems effectively to create the anticipated/needed results.

There is a difference between statistical data reporting to third party payors and data that will need interpretation, particularly if it is going to be used as part of managed care contract negotiations. Many third party payors and employers contracting with providers are overwhelmed with data. Therefore, each of the physicians and their medical practices need to understand the third party payor's need for specific information and respond to that need appropriately. Often, employers will ask managed care organizations and provider organizations to standardize data. Providers must comply with such requests but should not leave the interpretations of such standardized data to the third party or employer. *Interpretation of your data needs to be based on your understanding of your practice,* and hopefully your analysis can show that your practice pattern may generate long-term cost benefits to the employer group (e.g., patients return to work sooner, patients have fewer complications after surgery) even though the cost of the service might be higher because of the your practice pattern of keeping the patient in the hospital for an extra day for certain types of procedures/surgery.

Many employers/third party payors are developing their own provider profiling systems. They want to determine the average length of stay for given CPT-4 codes for their employees under the care of various doctors. They then combine profiling information with the average cost per day and make their conclusions about who they want to negotiate with in the future. Therefore, it is important that physicians analyze their own data and determine whether their patient population may be sicker, older, or require more care and have outcomes results that are appropriate for that patient population. Some companies, particularly in larger urban areas where an employer has a large workforce, have created sophisticated profiling systems. For example, the Harris Corporation of Melbourne, Florida, can now generate a report on every physician in its healthcare plan taking care of its employees. They can track the number of Harris patients treated, the amount paid to the doctor, the fifteen most common diagnoses and billing codes for their patients, and the number of hospital visits, inpatient, and outpatient surgeries, as well as lab and radiology volumes for their employee patients. It is in this kind of environment in which it is extremely important that each practice has its own computer system to ensure that the information that a company like the Harris Corporation gets is correct. It is important not only to ensure that the information is accurate, but to ensure that employers like the Harris Corporation are correctly interpreting that information.

BE READY FOR THE FUTURE

Medicare is now telling many physician practices that their Medicare intermediary will no longer respond to provider inquiries via mail. What other changes and new requirements from Medicare, and the hundreds of HMOs and PPOs, regarding electronic submission of claims/information will happen in the future is hard to predict. *What is easy to predict is that the future will hold more and more changes for physicians and their practices* along the lines that have been discussed in this chapter. This is just one more reason why physicians must approach their practices as businesses. It is understandable that after years of training, physicians want to "just practice medicine." However, neglecting important business activities and strategies often leads to practices that are no longer financially viable. Negotiating managed care contracts is going to become more and more a part of every physician practice. *Knowing what information is required, how to acquire that information, and how to analyze and use that information for successful negotiation of managed care contracts will continue to become increasingly important for all physician practices in the future.* Because many patients are "channeled" via their managed care contract to a given provider/provider location, being a "quality" physician today is no longer insurance for having a financially viable practice. This is often difficult for physicians to realize until their patients start requesting that their medical records be transferred to another practice as required by their new managed care contract.

This is economic reality today for physicians. This is what creates the need for change. The competition in some medical service areas where there is an oversupply of physicians becomes very competitive, particularly for being included in certain managed care contracts. It is in these competitive environments that having the right computer system, producing the right information, and analyzing it appropriately can make the difference between being part of a managed care system and successfully caring for patients under a given contract or not seeing those patients at all.

In addition to using your information generated by your computer system, you can also collect data and use it for your marketing. Marketing is another aspect of having the physician's practice being run as a business. If the physician practice has an annual budget, there should be an allocation for marketing. Such marketing can include, particularly in highly competitive marketplaces, the use of results from your outcomes studies. For example, some practices that specialize in treating female patients may even have a "women's health center," and some may market the fact that 80% of their female patients over fifty years of age have had a mammogram within the last twelve months.

The fact of the matter is that every marketplace is different and the information collected will therefore be different, based on payors' requests and the competitive nature of the marketplace. But regardless of the marketplace, the nature of the practice of medicine has become and will continue to become more and more business-oriented. As such, physicians and their practices need to understand the importance of using effective business tools designed for the healthcare industry and specific specialties/practices. The computer hardware/software, outcomes, and benchmarking are all parts of the changes that have taken place and that will continue to take place for a number of years to come in healthcare practices. The changes and recommendations given in the last two chapters are designed so that if implemented successfully, physicians can maintain financial viability. Assuming this happens, physicians will have the opportunity to use the recommendations in the rest of this book on how to use the revenues generated by the practice and those changes.

Financial Planning: From Home to Office and Back Again

Whatever your motives—helping others, healing the sick, pursuing science and knowledge, living up to your family's expectations, living up to your expectations, whatever—money was not likely close to the top of, if even on, the list of reasons by which you chose a career in healthcare. For most of us in healthcare, money was not, is not, and probably will not be the driving force to success in our relationships and our professional lives.

We measure their practice productivity, overhead, compensation, and benefits in dollars, the measure of money. The paycheck we take home from the practice pays for housing, food, cars, entertainment, insurance, debt retirement, mortgage payments, and all of the immediate needs, while hopefully meeting our expectations for educating our children and accumulating wealth for our retirement and our heirs; in essence, creating personal financial security. We measure and compare our income and net worth in dollars.

Everyone wants and desires a well-balanced personal and professional life. Everyone goes through various stages of growth and development. The compensation, in the form of cash and paid benefits, provides for your family lifestyle, now and in the future. The lifestyle you chose for yourself and your family depends in part on your compensation. And again, your compensation from the practice depends on your ability to steward the resources from your practice. Financial planning is the process by which you can organize your income and assets to meet your immediate needs, retire debt, increase net worth, and invest for future personal and family events. Financial planning is a process and depends on the stage we find ourselves in life, the reader may relate to experience of past events or expectations of events to come.

Financial planning services and products used to achieve planned events and meets goals are available through financial advisors, attorneys, accountants, and others, with varying levels of professional experience, knowledge, and skill. This book ends with a discussion of how to select and use professional advise with Internet addresses and access to tools you can use to achieve financial security both personally and professionally. First, however, the compensation and benefits available to you and your family through the practice, regardless of your status as employee or owner, are discussed.

THE PRACTICE LIFE CYCLE

Each practice goes through various stages (Figure 10–1). The practice that is just getting started, the emerging practice, is survival-oriented. In this stage, cash is tight. Revenue contracts are vital to securing short-term working capital needs. Receivables may not be sufficient to secure cash flow or loans. The practice needs a close working relationship with a banker. You, the practice owner, put in long hours and have to maintain a high degree of flexibility merely to survive. You have probably made it through this stage or are very close to making it through this stage and into the next stage, called the successful practice stage.

In the successful practice stage, you have established your clientele and revenue base, and you might even be saving some money. By this time in a practice's growth, procedures and systems have been implemented, taking away some of the flexibility that can be found in an emerging practice while providing

Practice Life Cycle

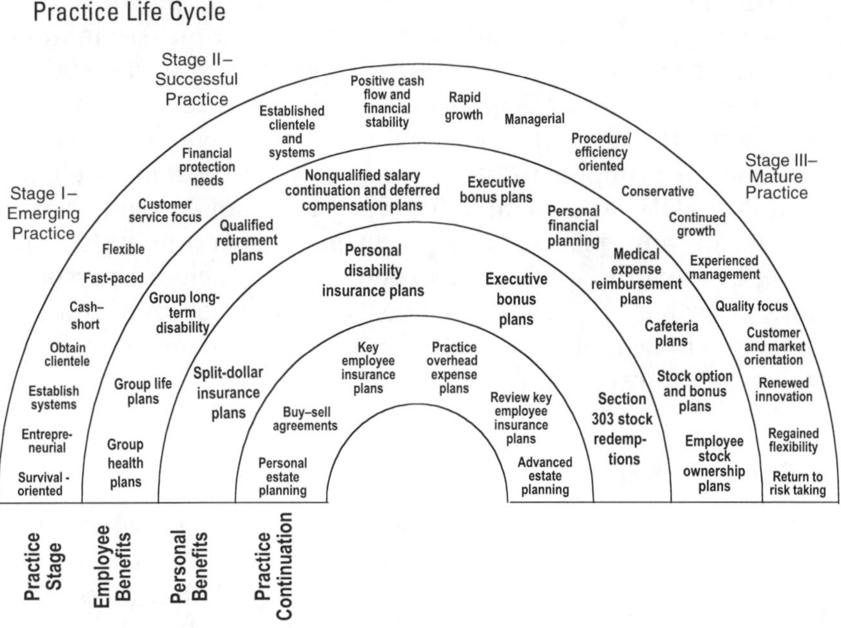

great stability in patient mix, research (if desired), and income streams. You have hired people to help with the three or four jobs that you were doing personally while in the emerging practice stage and now better appreciate administrative services in attending to the regulatory issues and monitoring of your employee or owner benefits.

Finally, there is the third stage: the mature practice. This is a stage of continued growth, although maybe not as fast paced as in the successful practice stage. The people you have hired have become experienced such that you do not have to keep a close watch on every detail of your practice—you have *established* people and *established* systems. You have more time to explore alternatives and have regained some of the flexibility in the hours you work, as well as in the tasks you decide to undertake. This may be a stage that you decide to take chances again on new products or new services. You may even decide to participate in an altogether new venture and let the practice take care of itself.

Different financial concerns and financial opportunities exist through the various practice stages; namely personal benefits, employee benefits, and practice continuation. Techniques that allow you to use your practice to provide you, the owner, with tax-favored benefits are examined in the discussion of personal benefits. The discussion of employee benefits explores areas such as group insurance plans, qualified retirement plans, and different types of nonqualified benefit plans. Finally, what happens to your practice when you are either unable or unwilling to continue working is explored. This includes personal estate planning, as well as practice valuation for continuation planning. This chapter can help you answer the question: What will happen to my practice when I'm not here?

PERSONAL BENEFITS

"I've put thirty years into this practice. It represents my lifetime of hard work. I don't want my time and effort wasted." "How can I get the most out of my practice for my family and myself?"

You've worked hard to get where you are today. You've traded each day in your practice for a dollar, or a hundred dollars, or a thousand dollars, or however much money you happened to make that particular day. Essentially, over the years, you have traded your lifetime for your estate and your practice. Now it's time to do something for yourself—to ensure that all you have worked for isn't wasted. And that takes planning. Planning can help you manage your practice dollars in three ways:

1. It lets you use practice dollars to provide personal benefits for you and your family, thus maximizing pretax dollars and income tax planning.
2. It helps you provide additional benefits to motivate and retain your key employees.

3. It helps keep your practice going should tragedy, such as disability, death, or property loss, strike unexpectedly.

Avoiding Double Taxation

Many practice owners take only enough money out of the practice to cover expenses because they want to keep money inside the practice to help it grow. If you want to take money out of your corporation, our tax system makes it difficult. If your practice pays a dividend, that money is taxed not once, but twice.

How does double taxation work? Your corporation pays the first tax on corporate income. If your corporation is in a 34% tax bracket and its earnings increase $10,000 this year, $3,400 will go directly to the federal government. Only $6,600 will be left for the corporation. If the corporation pays you the remaining $6,600 as a dividend, you pay a second tax—your personal income tax. If you're in a 36% tax bracket, the government will take 36%—$2,376. As a result of this double taxation, $5,776 (58% of your $10,000) has been used to pay federal taxes, and only $4,224 (42%) has been passed on to you. State personal and corporate income taxes take still more. The results are even more dramatic when the federal tax rates are higher. It's no wonder that many practice owners leave their money in the corporation! But that means they can't use the money for themselves or their families.

The challenge is to remove earnings from the practice in ways that avoid or reduce double taxation. It can be done by having your practice provide you with benefits that are either tax deductible to it or that are not income to you. Your corporation can provide you tax-favored benefits in several ways:

58% (More than Half!) Gone to TAXES!

- Through a Section 303 Redemption
- With "Split Dollar" insurance
- Under a Personal Disability Income Plan

A Section 303 redemption uses corporate dollars to pay your estate costs. "Split dollar" uses practice dollars to pay your personal life insurance. Personal disability income plans use corporate dollars to guarantee you an income if you cannot work.

At the time of your death, your corporation can pay your personal estate costs. A Section 303 redemption allows your corporation to provide dollars to pay your federal estate taxes, your state death taxes, your executor's and attorney's fees, your property management fees, and your funeral expenses. Best of all, this money is not taxed as personal income if you meet certain requirements.

Your practice corporation can also pay for your personal life insurance under a split dollar arrangement. You and your corporation enter into an agreement in which the corporation pays all or part of the premium on a life insurance policy on your life. The premium payments are styled as "loans." At your death, the insurance company pays a death benefit that is split two ways. The corporation receives enough of the death benefit to equal the "loans" or premiums it has paid. The rest of the death benefit is paid tax-free to your personal beneficiary. The bottom line is that your corporation recovers all its expenses while you have the benefit of personal life insurance. You will pay some taxes under this arrangement, but the cost is almost always less than paying the entire premium yourself.

Split dollar is particularly attractive when your practice is in a lower tax bracket than you are. It means your practice's after-tax dollars are cheaper than your after-tax dollars. Here's how: Assume, for example, that your annual insurance premium is $1,000 and you are in a 33% tax bracket, whereas your corporation is in a 15% tax bracket. Before you can pay the premium, you will need to pay income taxes on your earnings. In a 33% tax bracket, you must earn $1,493 to have $1,000 left over to pay the premium. Your corporation, on the other hand, must earn $1,177 to pay both the taxes and the premium. When your corporation's tax bracket is lower than your own, its dollars are "cheaper." In this example, the total cost of your life insurance could be reduced by $316 if your corporation paid the premiums through a split dollar plan.

You can use a split dollar plan as a fringe benefit for selected key employees as well. Unlike many other benefit programs, the split dollar plan lets you choose the employees you wish to reward. And your corporation will recover all its expenses while the employee's beneficiary receives the rest tax free.

BEING PREPARED IN THE EVENT OF BECOMING DISABLED

Your practice can also help you meet the single greatest threat to your personal and family security: disability.

In fact, 27% of all forty-five-year-old individuals will be disabled for ninety days or longer before they reach the age of sixty-five, and the odds of disability increase when people are considered in groups. If two forty-five-year-old people are in practice together, the chances of one of them experiencing a long-term disability before retirement is 46%. For three forty-five year olds, the odds of one of them becoming disabled increase to 61%. The odds are even higher for younger people. The average length of a disability is surprising. About one-third of all people now aged thirty-five will be incapacitated for three months or longer before they reach age sixty-five. The average length of a disability that lasts at least ninety days is two and a half years.[1]

> The odds of a person becoming disabled for ninety days or longer before age sixty-five are two to three times greater than that person's chance of dying.

These are shocking statistics. But what do they mean to you personally—and to your practice? Imagine that you have had an accident or a heart attack. Physical pain and rehabilitation aren't the only problems. Your income drops, but your expenses continue to climb as medical bills and doctor's fees are added to daily living costs. If your practice is unable to continue your salary, how will your family pay the bills?

---

[1] Minnesota Mutual & NALU. Based on 1995 morbidity tables.

Your practice can help with a disability income plan. Such a plan guarantees you an income when you are too disabled to work. It is paid for with deductible corporate dollars, which are not taxable to you. What's more, you do not have to give this benefit to all your employees; you can decide which employees receive it. Small wonder that this plan has been called the perfect personal fringe benefit.

EMPLOYEE BENEFITS

Employee benefits are your second planning opportunity. Today, benefit programs are almost taken for granted by both employers and employees. But they can be a powerful tool for motivating and retaining valuable people. Although benefits can be costly, replacing quality employees, whether because of retirement, death, disability, or a move, is even more costly in terms of recruiting, training, and providing orientation. More importantly, if you increase the tax-free benefits of certain employer-sponsored employee benefits, they become ordinary business expenses to the employer and nontaxable to the employee.

According to a recent United States Chamber of Commerce study, an average practice spends more than 40% of its payroll on employee benefits. The average cost of these benefits is more than $2.90 per payroll hour and almost $6,000 a year per employee. These figures show that businesses have a larger investment in their employees than they think. How about your practice? How much are you paying for your benefit programs? Careful planning can help you get the most out of those expenses—and just as important, can help you motivate and retain valuable employees.

Effective and cost-efficient employee benefits include qualified retirement plans, individual retirement accounts, nonqualified salary continuation plans, group term insurance, and executive bonus plans. Some of these benefits must cover most employees, but others can discriminate.

Qualified Retirement Plans

The most powerful company-wide benefit, the qualified retirement plan, creates retirement funds for loyal employees. Three important tax benefits make this plan cost-efficient to you and attractive to your employees: (1) your contributions are deductible, (2) your contributions grow tax-free within the plan, and (3) taxes to employees are deferred until payments or withdrawals are actually received.

To understand the tremendous effect of these tax advantages, let's work through a hypothetical example and compare a retirement program built by a qualified plan with one built by a personal savings or investment plan. If your practice increased your salary by $10,000, you could put the money in a savings or investment plan. However, if you are in a 28% tax bracket when you receive your salary increase, you will have $7,200 to invest after taxes. In contrast, a $10,000 contribution by the corporation to your qualified plan account is not reduced because all taxes are deferred until you begin receiving payments at retirement.

Now, assuming a hypothetical rate of return of 8% annually, the $7,200 in the savings plan will earn $576 in its first year. These earnings will again be reduced by personal income taxes at a 28% rate, leaving $415 after taxes. In this example, the qualified plan would earn $800 in its first year, which would not be reduced by taxes because the plan's earnings grow tax-free. After only one year, the qualified plan has earned $800 compared with $415 in the savings plan. Adding net contributions and net earnings together at the end of the first year, the difference between the two plans is significant. The savings plan totals $7,615, whereas the qualified plan has $10,800.

After twenty years of annual $10,000 contributions, the tax advantages become even more impressive: $494,000 in the qualified plan compared with only $299,000 in the savings plan. Of course, when money is withdrawn from the qualified plan at retirement, or by way of a withdrawal or loan, it will be taxed. But even after taxes, the qualified plan puts you $57,000 ahead of the savings plan! Which plan would you rather have?

Individual Retirement Accounts

Some businesses cannot afford a qualified plan. But owners and employees of these businesses can still get the tax benefits of a qualified plan with an individual retirement account, or IRA.

Some of the rules for IRAs have changed. However, contributions to an IRA still grow tax-free inside the account. Income taxes are deferred until payments are received at retirement. If the individual and the individual's spouse are *not* covered by a qualified plan, they can deduct the IRA contribution. (Effective in 1998, the Roth and Educational IRAs are options to certain income limits.)

In fact, your regular employees may receive a larger percentage of their salary in retirement income than you or your key employees do. That's "reverse discrimination." To illustrate how reverse discrimination works, let's work through the following example and compare the retirement benefits of three employees. One employee earns $15,000 a year, the second $75,000, and the third $125,000. At retirement, each employee receives a Social Security benefit, depending on age, length of employment, and other factors, up to a maximum of about $16,000 annually if retirement is at age sixty-five. As you can see, two of the employees in this example have reached the ceiling.

Now compare these Social Security benefits to the employee's salary. It's easy to see whom Social Security helps most. The $15,000 employee gets back nearly 50% of his or her salary in benefits, whereas the higher paid employees get back only 13 to 21% of their salaries. Benefits from a qualified plan don't make up the difference because a qualified plan cannot discriminate against rank and file employees. So even if we add qualified retirement benefits to this illustration, the higher paid employees still receive a lower percentage of their preretirement income.

Nonqualified Salary Continuation Plans

What can be done to bridge the gap seen with IRAs? A nonqualified salary continuation plan reverses reverse discrimination, providing additional retirement benefits to the selected key employees you want to reward, including yourself. The cost is minimal, and you do not need IRS approval.

A nonqualified salary continuation plan is an exchange of promises. The practice promises to provide disability, retirement, and death benefits, and the key employee promises to continue working for the practice for a specified period or until retirement. The extra benefits the practice pays act as "golden handcuffs" to keep key employees with the practice: The key employee can't afford to leave the firm and lose those benefits.

To make the plan work, you can create a tax-favored program or plan that pays the promised benefits to the key employee, and costs you little or nothing. There are two popular ways to provide insurance benefits for your employees: group term insurance and executive bonus plans.

Group Term Insurance and Executive Bonus Plans

You are probably familiar with the characteristics of low-cost group term insurance. In addition to the reasonable price tag, premiums are tax deductible to your corporation and employees are not taxed on benefits up to $50,000. Executive bonus plans can either supplement or substitute for group term insurance plans. Like group term, executive bonus plans provide low-cost protection, and premiums are deductible to your corporation. In contrast to group term, employees are taxed on the protection provided by an executive bonus plan, but the tax cost is usually small compared to the benefits provided.

These plans are especially attractive when the employee has a lower tax bracket than the corporation. Executive bonus plans have some additional attributes not shared by group term. They provide permanent, not temporary, protection. They can be offered on a completely discriminatory basis. That is, you pick and choose whom you want included in the plan. Executive bonus plans also avoid most government red tape, and they are easy and simple to administer.

These are the low-cost benefits you can provide your employees and yourself. They can free up a lot of after-tax personal income for their uses, while helping you motivate and retain your employees.

BUSINESS CONTINUATION

Business continuation—planning for the unexpected death of an owner or key employee—is the third planning area. There are three approaches to practice continuation: buy–sell agreements, key employee insurance, and personal estate planning.

Buy–Sell Agreements

Planning for death is distasteful; it reminds us that our days are numbered. That's why many people avoid this kind of planning. Unfortunately, failure to plan for death is nothing more than ignoring the inevitable. No financial plan is complete unless it considers and plans for the contingency of premature death.

A smart practice person plays the odds. Statistics show that if you are forty-five years old, you have a 19% chance of dying before age sixty-five. If you have a partner, there is a 34% chance that one of you will die before age sixty-five. If you have two partners, the odds are 47% that one of you will die before retirement.

If you die, what are your family's options in dealing with your practice? There are only two: They can sell the practice or they can retain it. If your partner dies, his or her family has the same two options. If you want your family to retain your practice, you must help them solve three common problems. First, who is going to run your practice if you leave the picture? There must be someone who can profitably manage it. This could be your spouse, a child, or a key employee. It could be anyone with experience in the practice's day-to-day affairs who is committed to staying for some time to come. Second, will your family be able to generate a steady income out of the practice? Your salary cannot be automatically continued to your spouse or children. They must perform valuable services to earn that salary. The only other source of money is a dividend, but unlike salaries, dividends are not deductible. Your practice probably could not afford to pay a salary if it wasn't deductible. Third, will your surviving partner be willing to cooperate with your family in running the practice? He or she will have to agree to pay a salary or a dividend so that your family has a regular income. (Remember that if he or she dies first, the shoe will be on the other foot. You will have to cooperate with your partner's spouse and children running the practice.)

If there is no one to run the practice, if your family cannot get money out of it on a deductible basis, or if your partner refuses to cooperate, your family will be in trouble. They may be better off selling the practice. Unfortunately, if your family decides to sell, they could have difficulty getting a fair price. First, the practice may not be as valuable because your death may have eliminated the primary reason for its success—you. Second, potential buyers may know your family must sell; consequently, they may offer less than what the practice is worth. Third, if you do not have a controlling interest in the practice, its value is decreased. A minority interest does not have the voting power to make practice decisions.

As you can see, your family must solve a variety of problems whether they retain your practice or sell it. Fortunately, there is an answer to these problems: a buy–sell agreement. This is nothing more than an agreement that directs what will happen to the practice at the time of your death. It takes the uncertainty out of transferring the practice and protects you, your partner, and your respective families.

If your partner dies and you survive, a buy–sell agreement avoids disputes between you and your partner's family. It allows you to take over the practice without taking in the surviving family as partners. It also prevents outsiders from purchasing your partner's interest and interfering in the practice's affairs. In short, the agreement smoothly transfers control to those people who will keep the practice going.

On the other hand, if you die and your partner survives, a buy–sell agreement ensures a market and a fair price for your stock. The agreement converts a nonliquid and otherwise unmarketable asset, your stock, into cash, which your estate can pass to your family. In addition, a properly drafted buy–sell agreement may establish a value of your practice for estate tax purposes. Here's how the buy–sell agreement works: You and your partner enter into a buy–sell agreement providing that when one of you dies, the remaining partner will buy the other's stock. If you die first, your family transfers your stock to your partner in return for cash. Sometimes the practice, rather than the surviving partner, will purchase the stock. But

More Than 95% of Businesses That Fail Do So Because of Managerial Incompetence or Inexperience!

either way the results are the same: The family receives cash, and the surviving partner gets the practice.

Key Employee Insurance

The profitable continuation of your practice can also depend on your key employees, especially on their managerial competence and experience. More than 95% of businesses that fail do so because they lack these two important qualities. Thus, a key employee's unexpected death can leave more than an empty chair; it can leave the practice in turmoil. Sales will be lost; credit may evaporate; practice contacts may disappear. Finding and training a replacement will be costly, and profits will fall. Like most practice owners, you probably ensure your tangible assets—vehicles, machinery, and buildings—but what about one of your most valuable assets—your key employees? Insurance is the best protection your practice can have against the loss of a key employee. Insurance on a key employee's life will provide cash to make up for lost sales and lost credit and to help you locate and train a qualified replacement.

Personal Estate Planning

Buy–sell agreements and key employee insurance are closely related to yet a third part of practice continuation: personal estate planning. This is planning that helps you manage, enjoy, and dispose of all your property according to your objectives. Your property includes the following:

- Your personal assets and real property
- Your practice assets
- Your life insurance
- Your other benefit programs

What happens to all this property at your death? It passes through an estate settlement process commonly called probate. This process supervises the transfer of assets from you to your heirs, and it can be expensive! Imagine that at the time of your death, all of your property is poured into a funnel for eventual distribution to your family. However, before your family receives a cent, many dollars may be drained away, by death taxes, income taxes, executor commissions, appraiser's fees, probate fees, accountant's fee, attorney's fees, and debts. These costs can add up! Between 30 and 60% of your estate may never reach the people you want to receive it. What's the solution to this problem? Planning. Planning can help you pass more property to your family.

Personal estate planning guards against the improper distribution of assets. Without such planning, assets may pass to unintended persons due to improper ownership designations, change of circumstances, or changes in the law. Personal estate planning guards against excessive transfer costs. It often reduces the size of the taxable estate, thereby reducing or postponing estate taxes. Personal estate planning also guards against lack of liquidity. If your estate doesn't have enough cash to pay settlement costs, your executor may have to sell some of your assets at a loss. Worse yet, your primary estate objectives may be thwarted. An obvious example would be if you had intended your family to continue your practice, but lack of liquidity forced your executor to sell all or part of it instead. Finally, personal estate planning guards against inadequate family income after death. It coordinates your life insurance, your benefit programs, your practice assets, and other income-producing properties to secure your family's future income.

To summarize, practice continuation tools include buy–sell agreements that protect you, your partner, and your families in the event of death; key employee insurance that helps you efficiently accomplish your lifetime goals; and personal estate planning. You have three planning opportunities to make your practice work for you: corporate dollars for personal benefits, employee benefits, and practice continuation plans.

Maximizing Compensation and Benefits from the Practice

Now let's address the ongoing concerns of the practice. We have discussed the issues around what happens if you or a partner/shareholder should die or become disabled for more than twelve months. We will again review these issues in more detail and then address the ongoing concern of the practitioner for current income and benefits through retirement.

Figures 11–1 through 11–3 provide an overview of the practice as employer and the consideration made for revenue sharing and benefits:

First, let's look at how you, the practice owner, can use dollars from your practice for personal benefits for you and your family. As discussed in Chapter 10, most business owners take only enough money out of the business to cover expenses because they want to keep money inside the business to help it grow. However, most professional practices take all the money out of the practice entity in the form of personal, taxable compensation to avoid double taxation.

If you want to take money out of your corporation, use your practice as a way to avoid or reduce double taxation. Have your

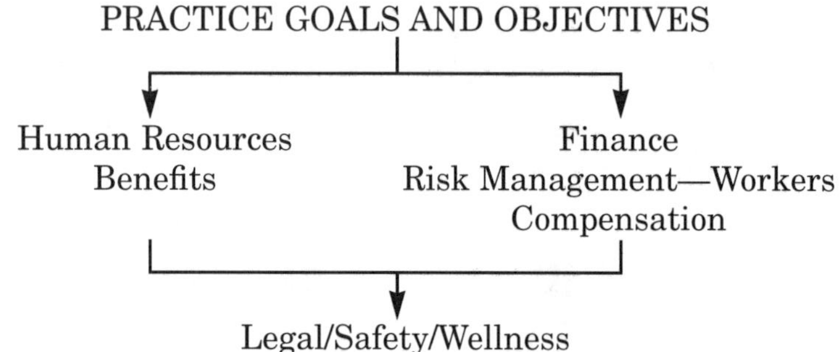

TOTAL TEAM COMPENSATION

Benefits	Compensation		
	Base	Bonus	Profit Sharing

Retirement	**Health & Welfare**	**Other**
Pension	Medical	Daycare
Profit Sharing Plan	Dental and Vision	Dependant's Health Costs
401(k)	Term Life	Flexible Savings Account
Retiree Medical	Group Disability Workers' Compensation	Long-Term Care Voluntary Benefits

practice provide you with benefits that are either tax deductible to it or are not income to you. Some options you have are a Section 303 redemption and a split dollar arrangement. Here is one way to structure split dollar premiums:

- The agreement provides that the employee owns the life insurance policy and pays premiums.
- The employer advances part or all of the premium.
- To provide security to the employer, the employee assigns the life insurance policy to the employer.
- Through the collateral assignment, employer receives back its premiums.
- The employee's beneficiary receives survivor benefits.

Alternatively, you may wish to structure split dollar arrangements as follows:

- An irrevocable trust is created.
- The trust purchases insurance.
- The practice and the irrevocable trust execute a split dollar agreement.
- Professional may gift term costs to trust.
- The practice pays insurance premium.
- The trust repays term cost to the practice.
- At the insured's death, insurance proceeds are paid to the trust and the practice.

During employment and the early life stages:

- Professional acquires policy.
- Professional and the practice execute an incentive split dollar agreement.
- The practice may bonus an amount equal to the term insurance cost to professional.
- The practice advances the balance of premium cost.

After retirement and in the later life stages:

- Premiums will be discontinued and the split dollar arrangement terminated.

- The practice may forgive the premium advances as compensation to the professional.
- The professional may use policy cash values to pay related income tax and to supplement retirement income.
- Estate planning considerations may dictate the policy be transferred to an irrevocable trust to provide estate liquidity.

Social Security is a structure to provide retirement income and certain health benefits to your employees. At retirement, each employee receives a Social Security benefit (depending on age, length of employment, and other factors) up to a maximum of about $16,000 annually if retirement is at age sixty-five. Highly compensated employees receive significantly lower percentage of their retirement income than the nonhighly compensated employees. Highly compensated employees, as defined in ERISA and regulated by the Department of Labor, are allowed to make up the difference in percentage of benefits to FICA taxable income by integrating the Social Security benefit with the contribution allocation inside qualified plans. However, benefits from a qualified plan don't make up the difference because a qualified plan cannot discriminate against rank and file employees. So even if we add qualified retirement benefits to our employer's mix of benefits, the higher paid employees still receive a lower percentage of their preretirement income.

A nonqualified salary continuation plan overcomes this apparent reverse discrimination by providing additional retirement benefits to the selected key employees you want to reward, including yourself. The following are some advantages of using nonqualified salary continuation plans:

- The limits on maximum benefits and contributions that apply to qualified plans do not apply to nonqualified plans. Therefore, nonqualified plans are often used to supplement qualified plans for selected employees.
- Benefits can be provided on a selective basis. The employer decides who will be covered. There is no requirement that benefits be shared with rank-and-file employees.

- There is no requirement that nonqualified retirement benefits be reduced for retirement before age sixty-two.
- Funds need not be placed in trust. Contributions remain an asset of the employer.
- There are no vesting requirements. Employees who terminate employment before retirement can, if you wish, forfeit their benefits. Nonqualified salary continuation benefits help tie key employees to your practice.

Investing in nonqualified salary continuation plans is advisable for the following groups:

- C-Corps earning more than $75,000
- Professional associations with taxable income
- S-Corp where the owner's tax rate is greater than the employee's tax rate
- Partnerships where the partner's tax rate is greater than the employee's tax rate
- Proprietorships where the owner's tax rate is greater than the employee's tax rate
- Any practice that has key people it would like to retain

CONSIDER FUTURE TAX RATES

As discussed in Chapter 10, you must plan for the continuation of your business in the event of your death or disability. Lack of planning may result in both your family and practice suffering.

We have already discussed the options that your family will have if you die and ways to ensure that both your family and practice are taken care of. One of the more advantageous arrangements is the buy–sell agreement. But what happens to your family and business if you are too disabled to work? You can enter into a buy–sell disability agreement. This is based on the same concept as the buy–sell agreement. A buy–sell disability agreement funded with a buy–sell disability contract can ensure you and your partners that money will be available to fund the purchase of your shares or partnership interest if you become disabled for more than twelve months.

A partnership is formed for business continuation and retirement accumulation:

- Agreement provides that upon death, interest transfers to survivors.
- Life insurance is specially allocated.
- Each partner buys a policy on the other.
- Add ASL riders for three or more owners.
- Only survivor shareholders may buy stock of deceased shareholder.
- If shareholders don't buy, corporation must redeem!

EMPLOYER-SPONSORED EMPLOYEE BENEFIT PLANS

Employee benefit plans, established for the welfare of all employees, are tax deductible to the corporation and not taxable to the employee on either premium basis or benefit-received basis. The number of employees in your practice determines applicability of additional laws and regulation of the benefits you offer your employees.

The Family Medical Leave Act, Americans with Disabilities Act, Department of Labor's regulator oversight acts of Employee Retirement Income and Security Act (ERISA) and COBRA, as well as the Internal Revenue Code and applicable state employment laws and regulation of health, life, disability, and workers compensation, all may affect your offering of plans to meet the needs and concerns of your employees.

In the best case scenario, we will have unlimited choice without discrimination. In addition to time off considerations for vacations and continuing education, we would provide sick days and leave without pay. But what measures can we take to provide economic security to our employees (and for ourselves as highly compensated employees) if the employee or his or her dependent is injured or ill and the employee requires extended time off? The risk issues are (1) the cost of insuring short-term income continuation of sick or injured employees and self-funding short-term income continuation for the welfare and benefit of all employees under IRC section 105, (2) the long-term income termination and replacement of income through group long-term disability income insurance, (3) healthcare costs and indemnification through worker's compensation insurance and healthcare insurance, and (4) life insurance on the employee and/or dependant in the event of death under IRC section 79.

Income security and protection would include (1) payroll deduction short-term disability insurance, (2) group short-term disability insurance, (3) group long-term disability insurance, and (4) group voluntary long-term disability insurance.

Dependant care expenses can be reimbursed under IRC section 129, making the high cost of dependant care more affordable. These plans include reimbursement of first dollar cost of child and elder care up to $5,000 per year, and long-term care insurance purchased as an individual contract at group rates.

If the employee is injured on the job, the employer is liable for all costs associated with returning the employee to work, including physician and hospital charges, rehabilitation costs, and income loss up to certain limits. The risk is borne entirely by the employer. The employer protects both the employee and employer through worker's compensation insurance.

Health insurance premium and costs of self-funding healthcare for the employee are tax favored to most employers and the benefit is not taxable in any case to the employee. In addition, the employer may provide a medical reimbursement plan for other costs of healthcare and wellness. Furthermore, the employer may allow the employee to purchase dependant coverage with before tax dollars through the flexible spending account.

Flexible spending accounts are established for the benefit and welfare of all employees. However, there are certain rules of participation and choice without discrimination to be followed. Again, the Department of Labor regulates certain benefits under ERISA and filed as 5500 forms. The Treasury Department regulates certain benefits under the Internal Revenue Code. Discrimination in favor of the highly compensated employees is prohibited and the fines severe. In addition, the employer is often held responsible for the first dollars used before the employee has funded the plan through salary reduction or out of pocket costs reimbursement. This aside, the significant benefits for you in designing flexible benefit plans that work for your employees are significant. You can benefit up to 125% of your average employee participation. The menu of choices may include the following:

- Term life insurance: payable to the employee's beneficiary, purchased in multiples of salary with first dollar premium up to the one year's salary to a maximum of $50,000 death benefit paid by the employer (IRC 79)
- Healthcare insurance or health maintenance organization premium paid for the employee and leveraged through the flexible spending account for the employee's dependent coverage premium
- Medical savings accounts and medical reimbursement plans: can be integrated to cover all healthcare costs an employee or their dependant might encounter
- Vision and dental coverage: often offered as a choice to the employees

Group short-term and long-term disability plans provide income loss security, but only for 60% of the employee's salary and only for limited duration. The employee may need higher limits of coverage, say 80% of current income and specific coverage for the employee's occupation and to age sixty-five. How disability premiums are paid determines when and if the benefit will be taxed. In general, if the premium is paid for by the employer, the benefit is taxed on receipt to the employee; if the employee pays the premium with before-tax dollars, the benefit is taxed; and if the employee pays the premium with after-tax dollars, the benefit is not taxed. Offering voluntary, individual contracts through the flexible spending account, paid for with after-tax payroll deduction, with simplified underwriting and priced at group rates, may be the most efficient means to purchase the coverage needed for each employee.

The cost of dependant care can be leveraged to include first dollar cost without first reaching the 7.5% of adjusted gross income threshold. IRC section 129 allows for reimbursement up to $5,000 per for dependant care.

Other benefits may also be added, including Pharmacy cards, long-term care insurance to cover employee or their dependants, health club memberships to promote wellness, expanded medical savings accounts, and added convenience of saving and financial planning. On a voluntary basis, even group auto and homeowner's insurance can be purchased as individual contracts on group rates.

Allowing the employee to choose or waive this coverage provides choice and provides the employee the ability to again pay premium or out-of-pocket expenses with before-tax, first dollar salary reduction, and to save taxes. As the employee, you benefit directly through the plans you choose for yourself and your family. And as the employer, you also benefit by savings in FICA tax on the reduced salaries. In all plans I have designed, the savings in FICA tax paid for the costs of design and installation of the flexible savings plan and voluntary benefit plan.

Disclaimer

This material is intended to be informative to owners of professional practices and is designed to motivate them to improve their personal and practice financial plans. All parties reviewing this text must look to their own tax and legal counsel for specific advice applying these ideas to their own particular circumstances. A knowledgeable attorney should draft documents implementing these ideas. North Star Resource Group is one of the principal financial services firms in the nation. Because of North Star's unique structure, we are able to make available an insurance brokerage, a security brokerage, and investment advisory services, which bring our clients the products, services, and consultation that will truly benefit them. Please refer to our website at http://www.northstarfinancial.com for the complete list of our services and full disclosure of our people, relationships, and credentials.

12

Retirement Planning: How to Arrange for and Coordinate Income from Multiple Sources

Leave your retirement to chance! If you plan on winning the lottery, then you never have to worry about having enough for retirement. Or if you plan on being one of the 36% unlucky people who die young, then of course you need not plan for financial independence at retirement. On the other hand, if you plan on retirement, achieve financial independence, and practice your own advice of leading a healthful lifestyle, you and your spouse or domestic associate will be comfortable and not dependent on others. Establishing an estate plan is presented in Chapter 15. First, let's look at the retirement planning process.

There are six elements that you need to establish a sound retirement plan. First, you need to determine your savings personality. You will need to know your risk tolerance and appropriate asset allocation mix to best put together a program that will work for you. Second, you will need to identify how much you need to save now to meet your retirement goals. Third, you will need to explore the different sources of retirement income from Social Security to qualified retirement plans to your personal savings. Fourth, you will need to look at the different types of employer-sponsored retirement plans. Fifth, you will need to look at IRAs to determine whether they are right for you. Sixth, you will need to explore your personal savings and the different investment vehicles that are available. And finally, you will need to put all of this together so that you will have a good idea of what you want to accomplish and how you plan to attain that goal.

DETERMINING YOUR SAVINGS PERSONALITY

Many of us have a glorified idea of retirement. We think of traveling to warm, sunny locations. We think of retirees on the golf course. We think retirement is a worry-free time for most people's lives. However, for many people, retirement creates a set of financial burdens that, unless properly planned for, can postpone retirement, or certainly make retirement not live up to our expectations.

The first piece of our puzzle is to understand your savings personality. There are four basic types of savings personalities: planners, strugglers, deniers, and impulsives. *Planners* sit down and think through retirement and have made it a point to alter their current lifestyle, if necessary, to put money away toward a retirement nest egg. *Strugglers* are people who are not willing to make the lifestyle changes necessary to reach their retirement goals. These are people who have trouble finding money to save. *Deniers* typically spend everything they make and think that their pension and Social Security will provide plenty of money for a comfortable retirement. Often, these people have not taken the time to sit down and work out just what they will need in monetary terms to have a retirement that lives up to their expectations. Much like the deniers, our fourth personality type are the *impulsives*. Impulsives live for today and don't think about tomorrow. Impulsives think that they have plenty of time to think about retirement and plenty of time to start saving—later, not today.

Which one of these are *you*? If you think you may be a struggler, denier, or an impulsive, you will need to work against your natural inclinations if you want to be prepared for a comfortable retirement. If you fall into one of the categories other than planners, you're not alone. The different personality types are split fairly evenly among the different classifications. Once your personality type is determined or a plan has been created to overcome some of the personality obstacles that you face, the next step is to identify how much you will need for a retirement that will live up to your expectations.

DETERMINING HOW MUCH TO SAVE

In many cases, you will be surprised to find out how much it is really going to take to prepare for retirement. Once a dollar amount that will allow you to retire comfortably has been determined, the key is not to be overwhelmed if that turns out to be a relatively large number. Planning early gives you time to break that number down into manageable amounts that can be put away over the rest of your working years.

When you look at just how long you will be living without a paycheck, the number of years in retirement is often almost as many years as you've spent working. At age sixty-five, one in four men will live to be age ninety. Whereas two of every five sixty-five-year-old women will live to be age ninety. If we look at a married couple, each age sixty-five, the probability is at least 55% that one of the two will be alive at age ninety.

When trying to determine the amount you will need at retirement, there are a couple of important considerations: (1) expenses, (2) average percentage of current income needed, and (3) inflation. First, some expenses that you currently have will be eliminated by the time of retirement. In most cases, your house is paid for. Often, the amount of money you will need to spend on clothes decreases. Second, for most people, the average percentage of current income that is needed for a comfortable retirement is approximately 75%. A couple making $80,000 per year before retirement will need about $60,000 to keep their current style of living. The third factor to consider is inflation. Although some expenses will decrease in retirement, those expenses that remain through retirement will most certainly be affected by inflation. Think back to the first car you purchased or the first home you bought. If we could find a deal like that today, we'd snap it up in a minute! Housing as an investment has appreciated at about 10% per year for the past thirty years! Unfortunately, so has replacement property. Today, we enjoy the lowest mortgage rates in more than fifty years, and refinancing may be a prudent move, but only if the monies are needed for other debt retirement. Again, the goal is to have the mortgage paid off by the first day of retirement.

So, back to the question, "How much will I need?" The answer is going to depend on a number of factors. More specifically, the question is, "How much will I need to personally save, such that when that is added to my qualified retirement plans and Social Security benefit, I have the ability to reach the goals that I've set for my retirement?"

PERSONAL INVESTMENTS

Depending on your income and qualified retirement plans available, you may need additional investment plans to reach your retirement goals!

The answer to the question, "How much do I need to save for retirement?" is an exercise that must be done individually. In addition to the factors already discussed, you also need to examine the time you and your spouse have to save for retirement, the age at which you expect to retire or want to retire, and how long you will need your retirement income to last.

There are three major sources of retirement income: (1) Social Security, (2) nonqualified retirement plans, and (3) qualified retirement plans or pensions.

Social Security

Some people believe that Social Security will take care of all of their retirement needs. Others are concerned that it won't be enough. Still, others are concerned that Social Security may not be there at all! Social Security is a consideration, and it will be up to you to determine how much you are willing rely on Social Security being there and to determine what portion of your retirement income Social Security will cover.

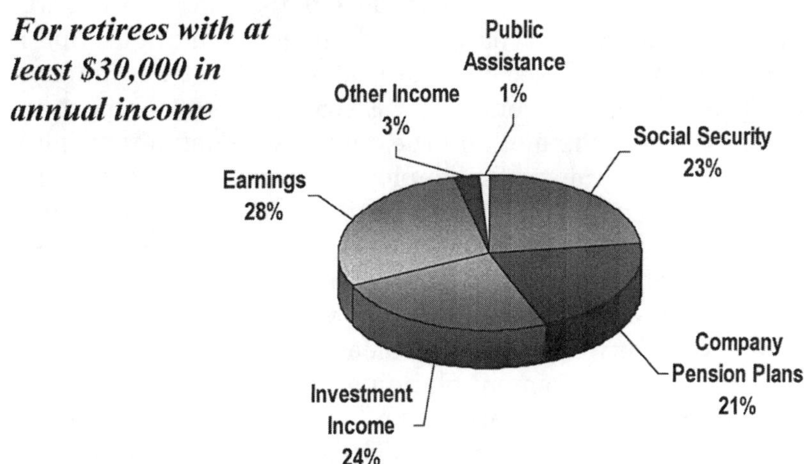

Sources: Social Security Administration, 1996; and Administration on Aging. "A Profile on Older Americans: 1996."

According to the most recent census, more than one-third of all individuals over the age of sixty-five live on an annual income of less than $10,000. That's a surprising statistic, isn't it? One-third of those in retirement are living near the poverty line! At the other end of the spectrum, less than 7% have incomes of $50,000 or more. Perhaps you planned adequately for your retirement and are now enjoying a comfortable one. And even if you are just beginning to plan, there are strategies you can implement to improve your lifestyle and get the most out of your retirement years.

First, Social Security provides a smaller portion of most people's retirement income than they might expect (Figure 12–1). Only 23% of their income comes from Social Security. Another 21% comes from pension plans, and a whopping 52% comes from part-time jobs (earnings) and personal savings and investments.[1]

Another surprise for most people is that many retirees have to take part-time jobs to help provide for about half of their

---

[1] Social Security Administration, 1996.

annual income. In fact, approximately 3.8 million Americans aged sixty-five and older are working, representing about 12% of all seniors. And 46% of these workers are holding full-time jobs.[2]

Providing access to financial planning services for the employees, including yourself, can be a bonafide benefit in that the service assists all employees in developing plans to ensure a comfortable retirement, payment of current obligations, and reduction of stress caused by financial uncertainty. In addition, the education requirement under ERISA and other Department of Labor oversight is met and the employer benefits through increased participation in the employer-sponsored benefit plans.

By putting your company's retirement savings plan to its best use, you can help increase the portion that your pension contributes to your total annual income at retirement. This, in turn, can reduce the probability that you'll have to work to supplement your retirement income needs.

As a part of retirement planning, you can file a request with the Social Security administration to determine what your benefits from that program will be. The benefits that will be projected are for a "normal" retirement age. We must keep in mind that for those expecting or wanting to retire before age sixty-five, the benefits will be reduced significantly.

For people on the lower end of the income scale, Social Security may provide a significant source of retirement benefits. For example, a retiree who was making about $15,000 per year will have a Social Security benefit that is close to 40% of his or her income while working. On the other hand, for the person who was making about $100,000 per year, Social Security will provide only 10% of that person's preretirement income.

Two final points on Social Security. First, it is not designed to provide *all* necessary retirement income. Second, the higher your pay has been, the greater your retirement income "shortfall."

Nonqualified Retirement Plans

Many investment options are available in which to invest your retirement dollars: annuities, municipal bonds, mutual funds, stocks, real estate, and practice interests are among a few.

[2] Administration on Aging, "A Profile on Older Americans: 1996."

Unlike qualified plans, your nonqualified retirement plan has no limits! You can put money into your nonqualified plan, and you can take money out of your nonqualified plan without worrying about IRS rules and regulations. However, there may be administrative fees and expenses imposed by the plan administrator.

EMPLOYER-SPONSORED RETIREMENT PLANS

Qualified Retirement Plans (Pensions)

The final source of retirement income is qualified retirement plans or your employer-provided pension. If an employer-sponsored qualified plan is available to you, it probably makes sense to take advantage of it. This chapter discusses some of the qualified plans that are available, including defined benefit plans and defined contribution plans, which include your profit sharing or 401(k) plans, the new SIMPLE plans, tax-deferred annuities, and simplified employee pensions (SEPs).

Let's take a look now at each type of qualified retirement plan on an individual level starting with defined benefit plans.

Defined Benefit Plans

As the name implies, defined benefit plans specify a benefit that will be paid to you at retirement. Often, this is based on a formula that may consider your final average salary and your years of service. It may be offset by Social Security benefits. A typical defined benefit plan promises you a flat, monthly amount to be paid over your lifetime or the lives of you and your spouse. Typically, defined benefit plans are funded completely by your employer. Most people refer to these types of plans as their pensions from work.

Defined Contribution Plans

Defined contribution plans, on the other hand, define the contribution and not the benefit. The benefit to be received at retirement is a function of how much you put in, how often you contribute to this type of plan, and the earnings on these plans over your working years.

There are a number of different types of defined contribution plans. You may hear them called money purchase pension plans, profit sharing plans, 401(k) plans, or ESOPs (employee stock ownership plans).

A money purchase plan is usually funded by contributing a fixed percentage of your compensation to a qualified plan. There are limits, however, in how much you can contribute; at most, 25% of your salary (and even that figure is capped) at a top contribution of $30,000 per year.

Profit sharing plans are somewhat more flexible than the other types of defined contribution plans. Contributions to these plans are often based on profits or profitability of the sponsoring company. In some years, no contributions will be made to a profit sharing plan. As with the money purchase plan, there are limits on the amounts that can be contributed to this type of plan. The maximum contribution under a profit sharing plan is up to 15% of your salary, and again, that figure is capped at $30,000 annually. More and more, profit sharing defined contribution plans are allowing employees who are participants in the plan to direct the investment of many contributions to these types of plans. They allow the employees to choose between a number of pooled investments in which to invest their specific account under this plan.

The 401(k), or salary savings plans, are another form of defined contribution plan. In these plans, the employee typically defers a portion of his or her salary rather than relying solely on company contributions to fund the plan. As with the other types of defined contribution plans, the deferrals are not taxed until they are withdrawn. In most situations, the participant has the option of directing where the money will be invested within his or her specific account.

ESOPs, or employee stock ownership plans, are a final type of defined contribution plan. These plans are less common than the types of plans already discussed. ESOPs are defined contribution plans that are invested primarily in the stock of the company sponsoring the plan. In an ESOP, the participants investment choices are somewhat limited in that most of the contributions are allocated to stock in that specific company. Again, professional practices are limited with regard to whom may own its stock. Consequently, ESOPs are not common in most states. However, you may establish an ESOP for you and your employee if you are engaged in related businesses of treatment or therapies that are marketed under a separate name from the practice.

A new type of plan has recently become available. It was created under the Small Business Job Protection Act of 1996. These SIMPLE plans, standing for savings incentive match plan for employees, are attractive to small businesses because they carry very low administrative costs as long as they follow a government-approved prototype. These SIMPLE plans are available as 401(k)s or IRAs, and like 401(k)s, they allow employees to defer a portion of their salaries on a pretax basis.

The tax-sheltered annuity or tax-deferred annuity, also called a 403(b) plan, is another qualified savings plan. This type of plan is available for employees of nonprofit organizations and some government organizations. These plans allow employees to make pretax contributions of up to 20% of salary, this figure being capped at $9,500 per year.

The final type of plan is a simplified employee pension, or an SEP plan. An SEP plan is much like a profit sharing plan in that contributions are very flexible; however, these contributions are placed into IRAs that are chosen by the employees. The SIMPLE plan replaces the SEP plan option for new plans. However, if your practice had established an SEP or salary reduction SEP or SAR-SEP, you may continue these plans without converting to a SIMPLE plan. The SEP and SAR-SEP plans provide higher maximums on annual contributions and have less restrictive highly compensated rules and testing.

With all of the different types of qualified plans, the contributions made to the plans are made on a pretax basis, meaning you are not taxed on the dollars as they go into the plan. Each of these plans also has tax-deferred growth within the plan. However, the government will not allow you to escape taxation entirely. You are merely postponing the payment of tax.

Distributions from qualified plans will be taxed at ordinary income rates. Money that is left in the plan and not distributed by the participant still continues to enjoy the tax deferral even after retirement. Even though you are taxed on distributions from qualified plans, there may be some tax advantages available depending on what type of distribution is made. Whether it's a lump sum distribution, meaning you are taking a distribution of the entire balance in your account, tax advantages may also be available depending on when money was contributed to a qualified plan.

Employer matching, which is available with some types of qualified plans, was touched on briefly. Another way to look at an employer match is that it represents an immediate return on your investment. For example, if your plan says that your employer will match your contributions 50¢ on the dollar (up to 4% of compensation), for each dollar you put in up to the 4%, you have an immediate 50% return in addition to the other tax advantages of the qualified plans.

Pulling the qualified plan information together is difficult to do in general terms because there are so many different types of plans. You should find your *summary plan description*, which your employer should have provided to you, and read through it. Second, make the most of the opportunities available with qualified plans. Think of it as paying yourself first. Often, we pay all of our bills and whatever is left we get to keep. A better approach may be to operate under the mind-set that you are going to pay yourself. Of course, leaving enough left over to pay those other bills. Third, because many plans have a waiting period before an employee can enroll, if you are planning to take advantage of a qualified plan, try not to hop from job to job. People who change jobs frequently find themselves unable to contribute to qualified plans because of the waiting period. Finally, if you own your own practice, consider establishing some sort of tax-qualified retirement plan. Insurance companies typically offer plans that are very cost-effective and easy to establish and administer even for the smallest of businesses.

IRAs

Fifth on our list of retirement planning strategies is to understand where IRAs fit. Individual retirement accounts, or IRAs, are very popular retirement savings vehicles. Contributions of up to $2,000 may be made on a tax-deductible basis to an IRA depending on your eligibility for other qualified retirement plans and your income level. Even if the contributions are not deductible up front, the earnings in these accounts grow tax deferred until you withdraw the funds.

So, should you set up an IRA? Tax law changes have affected many people's ability to deduct IRA contributions. Whether your contribution is deductible may influence your decision on setting up and contributing to an IRA. If you are not an active participant in a qualified retirement plan, you are eligible to deduct your entire IRA contribution, regardless of your income level. If you are an active participant in your employer's retirement plan, the income tax deduction for IRAs is completely phased out when an individual's modified adjusted gross income reaches $35,000. For a married couple, the deduction is phased out at $50,000. Remember, even nondeductible contributions to an IRA still give you the opportunity for tax-deferred growth. However, if your employees are not able to contribute to an IRA and you are not able to make maximum contributions to your qualified profit sharing or pension plans, both you and your employees are disadvantaged to reach your retirement goals.

Can you have an IRA? Well, the answer to that question is, "Yes," if you have earned income and are younger than seventy and half years of age. Anyone with earned income can contribute to an IRA up to $2,000 or the total of your earned income, whichever is less.

The Small Business Job Protection Act, mentioned earlier, also made some changes to the rules for IRAs beginning this year. The new rules allow a full contribution and deductibility of that contribution for any monies placed in an IRA for the benefit of a nonworking spouse. As with all qualified plans, any distributions made before you turn fifty-nine and a half years of age are subject to an additional 10% penalty tax in addition to the regular tax on the distribution. For distributions from IRAs, if they are made to pay medical expenses and those expenses exceed 7.5% of your adjusted gross income, the penalty tax will not apply. Finally, if you become unemployed, you may take distributions from an IRA to pay medical insurance premiums without the 10% penalty tax.

PERSONAL SAVINGS

The sixth strategy for a successful retirement plan is to maximize the dollars that you put away for retirement. With all of the different messages from the media, you might think that you need to examine hundreds of investments before you understand what to expect from an investment. We will explore the "basic three":

1. Equity
2. Fixed income investments
3. Money market investments

Virtually all investments are composed of one or some combination of these three.

As a part of the retirement planning process, you need to determine your risk–reward propensity. Some types of investments have a very high market risk. This means that the value of the investment fluctuates considerably. Past experience shows us that these more volatile types of investments (e.g., stocks) provide the largest gains over long periods.

Funds with low market risk are those that do not vary widely and often carry a different type of risk—inflation risk. Money market funds, for example, do not vary in price on a day-to-day basis; however, a low risk investment of this type typically also provides a lower reward. The earnings on a money market account may not keep up with inflation.

How do you know if you are comfortable taking risk? And how much risk should you take? If you are willing to accept some short-term losses, with the idea that you may realize larger gains over the long term, you may feel comfortable investing in more volatile investments.

Again, as part of the retirement planning process, you need to determine your investment personality (Figure 12–2). You may want to consult an expert who can help structure a portfolio that will attempt to provide the most gain, yet living within your risk tolerance. The MAPs program is covered in Chapter 15.

Equities

When people think of equities, they typically think of common stocks, but equities also include real estate, oil and gas, and pre-

Build a Portfolio Which Matches Your "Personal Profile"

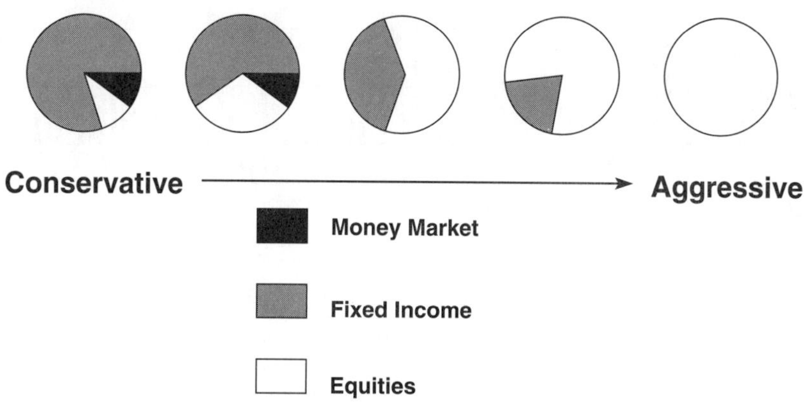

cious metals. The major advantage of investing in equities is that historically equities have provided a greater return. Some disadvantages of investing in equities are that there is market risk associated with investing in equities because they can widely fluctuate over the short term. Equities also may not provide sufficient current income to meet your needs. Most equities carry the potential for long-term growth at the expense of providing current income. In addition, because they carry this potential for long-term growth, they may be relatively illiquid.

Many people think of the stock market as a place where people lose money. Investors who bought and kept their investments experienced gains, over the long haul. Two of every three years, the stock market has tended to be up. This is another way of looking at investment returns, over time. The S&P 500 Index, an index often used when referring to stock market returns, tends to perform well over longer holding periods (Figure 12–3).

If investors in equities hold on to their investments for long periods, some of the fluctuation is taken out of this type of investment. Between 1926 and 1997, if we look at the stock market on a one-year period, in three of every ten years, the market

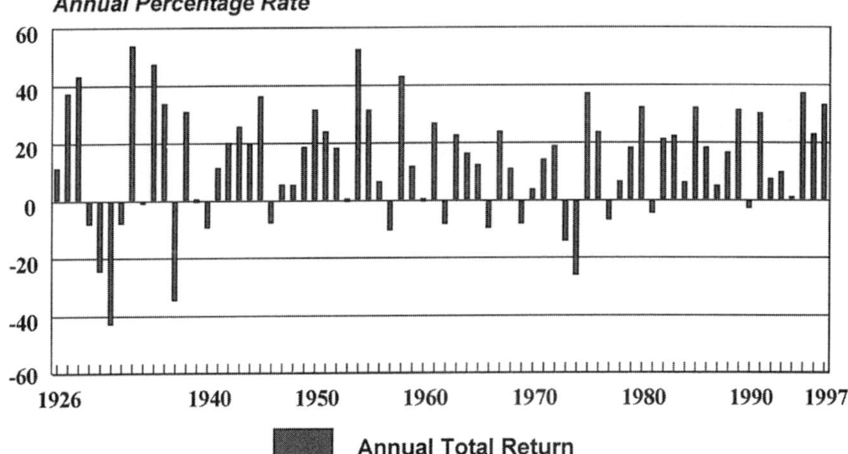

* Past performance is no guarantee of future results.

Sources: © Computed using data from *Stocks, Bonds, Bills and Inflation 1998 Yearbook* ™ Ibbotson Associates, Chicago (annual update work by Robert G. Ibbotson and Rex A. Sinquefield). Used with permission. All rights reserved.

has been down. If we look at a ten-year period, however, 97% of the time, the market has been up over any given ten-year period.

Over a one-year period, the most volatile investment would be small company stocks, with potential high returns and potential high losses! When you look at this same asset class over a longer time horizon, however, the range of gains and losses become narrower. Thus, having the courage to hold on to investments when they go down can be rewarded with gains, if you have the courage and fortitude to "hold" your investment for long periods.

Fixed Income Investments

The second broad asset class is fixed income investments.

Primarily, when we think of fixed income investments, we think of bonds. Another way to think of bonds is that you have loaned money to a corporation or to the government, and the bond represents that company's or government's promise to repay you. Fixed income investments also include mortgage-backed securities, long-term CDs, fixed annuities, and even the cash value of traditional life insurance policies.

The major advantages of fixed income investments are that they can typically provide a higher current income than many types of equities and money market investments, they have lower investment risk than equity investments, and there may be some potential tax advantages such as with municipal bonds.

Disadvantages of fixed income investments include a very limited capital growth potential and an exposure to purchasing power or inflation risk.

However, recent years have provided fixed income investors with some of the highest returns ever experienced in these assets.

Money Market Investments

The final investment option is money market investments. Money markets primarily consist of short-term debt instruments such as commercial paper and treasury bills and short-term savings such as CDs and bank savings accounts. The major advantage of money market investments is that they are very safe and very liquid.

A disadvantage of money market investing is that there is almost no growth potential. This is coupled with a large degree of purchasing power risk. Because money market investments are very liquid, they typically provide a lower level of current income than can be found over longer-term investments.

The returns on money market (T-Bills), fixed income, and stocks have varied significantly over time. Over longer periods, historical return relationships have remained quite consistent, with small company stocks leading the way, followed by large company stocks and corporate and government bonds and T-bills (Figure 12–4).

Pooled products as an alternative to direct securities investments include investments such as the following:

- Mutual Funds
- Annuities

STOCKS, BONDS, T-BILLS AND INFLATION: 1925 - 1997

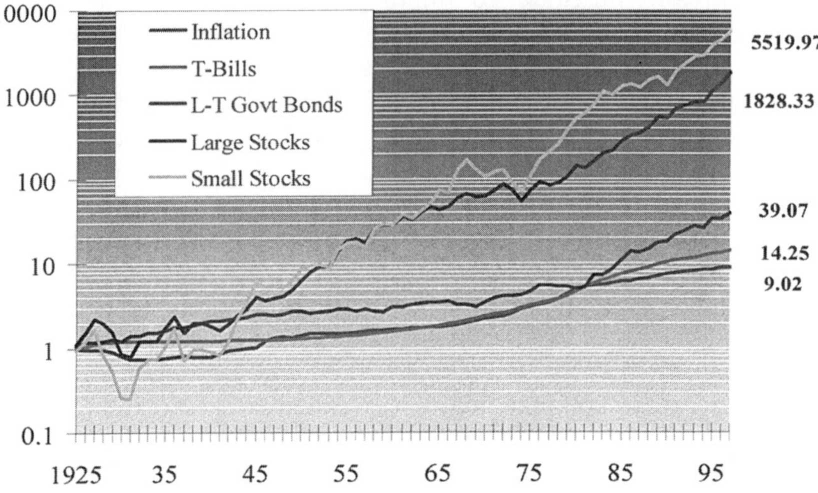

* Assumes reinvestment of income and no transaction cost or income taxes. This is a hypothetical example for illustrative purposes only. Both Government Bonds and T-Bills are guaranteed as to the timely payment of principal and interest, offer a fixed rate of return if held to maturity, and are insured by the U.S. government.

The values of equity investments are more volatile than other securities. The value of small company stocks is more volatile than large company stocks.

Source: © Computed using data from *Stocks, Bonds, Bills and Inflation 1998 Yearbook* ™ Ibbotson Associates, Chicago (annual update work by Robert G. Ibbotson and Rex A. Sinquefield). Used with permission. All rights reserved.

Pooled products reduce risk through:

- ◆ Diversification
- ◆ Professional Security Selection and Management
- ◆ Access to Dollar-Cost-Averaging

Investing

A common sense approach to investing in any asset class is to start with a quality base, then to move to aggressive investments. Too often, this common sense approach has been ignored by new investors.

Have you ever wondered if *now* is the right time to buy or sell? Well, if you can identify with this thinking, you need to understand a thing or two about market timing. Some investors are tempted to time the market as though this is a guessing

FIGURE 12–5

An Example of Dollar Cost Averaging

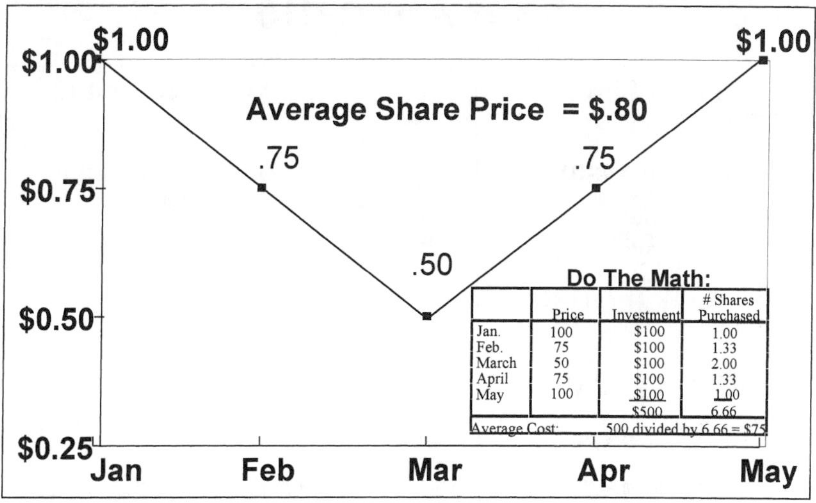

Do The Math:

	Price	Investment	# Shares Purchased
Jan.	100	$100	1.00
Feb.	75	$100	1.33
March	50	$100	2.00
April	75	$100	1.33
May	100	$100	1.00
		$500	6.66
Average Cost:		500 divided by 6.66 = $75	

* Dollar cost averaging does not guarantee a profit or insure against loss in a declining market. Also, because such a program involves regular investment purchases regardless of fluctuation price levels of the investment, consider your financial ability to continue purchases through periods of low price levels.

game. What happens when you guess wrong? By guessing wrong only thirty months out of the last seventy-one years, you could lose most of the return in stocks!

When you invest fixed sums of money at set intervals (e.g., monthly, quarterly), you are able to buy shares at an average cost less than the average price. Dollar cost averaging does not guarantee a profit or insure against loss in a declining market, but it does enable you to buy low and avoid investing at the top of the market. However, because such a program involves regular investment purchases regardless of fluctuation price levels of the investment, consider your financial ability to continue purchases through periods of low price levels (Figure 12–5).

Asset allocation may be used as a strategy to help minimize risk and enhance return. Allocation of investments may provide for an overall return that is greater than a single investment (Figure 12–6).

Illustration of The Benefit of Asset Allocation

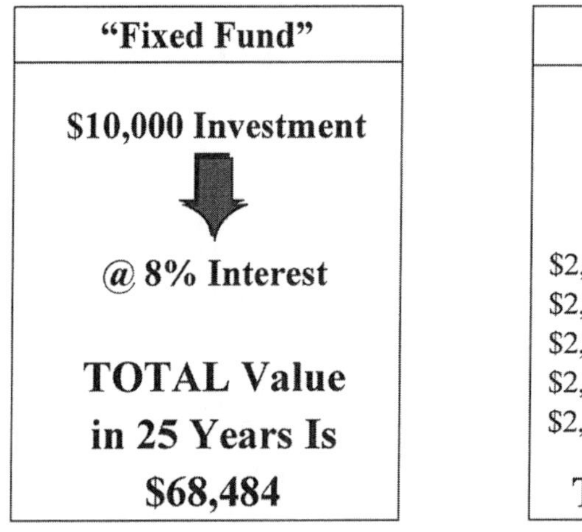

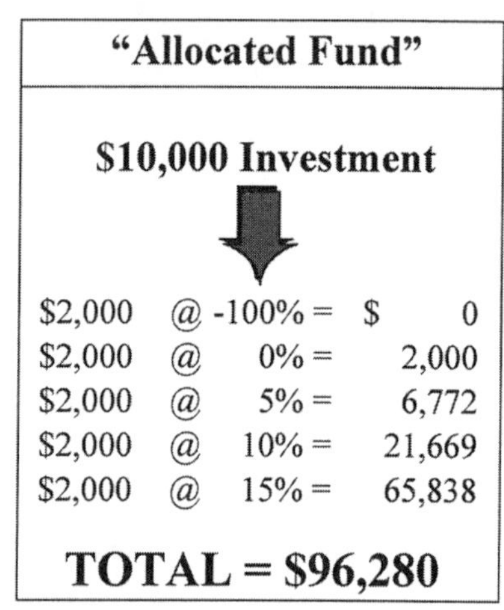

* Rates of return are hypothetical and for illustrative purposes only.

Some investments have a low correlation to each other. Simply put, correlation is a measure of how a particular asset will react to certain market conditions in relation to another investment. Stocks and bonds tend to react differently to market events. By using both assets, which are not closely correlated, an investor can *reduce risk*.

Another risk reduction strategy is to diversify—outside of the United States. International investing will play an increasingly important role in providing opportunities to investors. By diversifying assets beyond United States–held companies, it is possible to *reduce risk*, and enhance return.

WHAT IS THE "BEST" PORTFOLIO?

The "best" portfolio for you could cause someone else to lose sleep at night. This process should take into account your personal goals and preferences, as well as an assessment of your existing holdings.

Let's assume that you have decided to start seriously saving for retirement. Great! But you know, as you think about

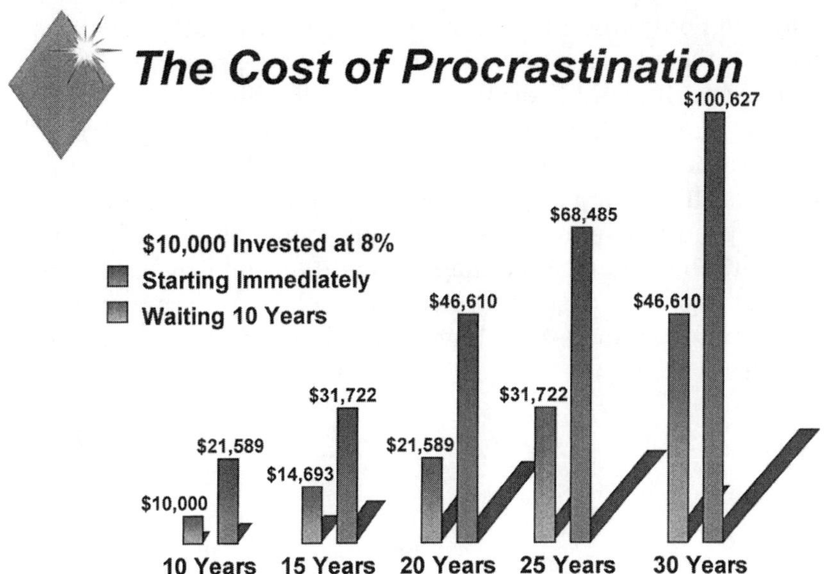

* This is a hypothetical example and rate of return for illustrative purposes only.

it, you have other obligations and demands on your money that could keep you from saving. Let's take a look at the difference starting early can make in retirement planning. Saving $1,000 for ten years, if given enough time to grow, can exceed a $34,000 investment! And returns experienced in recent years have tended to be higher than historic averages.

We all know that procrastination can take a toll on getting almost anything done. When it comes to retirement savings, the loss of just one year of annual savings of $1,000 can cost you at retirement time. In this example, the difference is $17,449 in accumulations—just for delaying action for one year!

Procrastination costs money. It simply doesn't pay to put off your financial plans, particularly when it comes to retirement planning. Let me show you what I mean.

After reading this chapter, you may immediately begin taking concrete steps toward achieving your financial goals. Or, you may wait quite a while before doing much of anything. Let's assume that you decide to invest $10,000 at 8% right away (Figure 12–7). Thirty years later, you will have earned, $100,627. But, if you had waited ten years before investing the same $10,000, you would have earned only $46,610. That's a difference of more than $54,000! Of course, this is a hypothetical illustration only, and its performance is not indicative of any particular investment. However, don't put off preparing for your retirement. It could literally cost you a fortune.

We have looked at the six retirement planning strategies that are necessary for you to consider to plan a successful retirement. If your savings personality is not that of a planner, you should probably take steps to become more "planning" oriented.

Although there is no magic formula or one right answer in putting together a sound retirement plan, you can make the most of the resources you have available so that you can afford to retire.

13 CHAPTER

Risk Management and Risk Transfer Vehicles

DISABILITY INSURANCE

How Likely Are You to Become Disabled?

What are the chances you will be hit by a car? Perhaps it will never happen to you. Only one of every eight people will be in an automobile accident this year. And, of course, only a small percentage of those people will have disabling consequences! Nonetheless, probability theory being what it is, your chances are greater than zero. Depending on where your live and practice, your chances may be much greater than zero. The medical care and disability income replacement under your auto/homeowners insurance is minimal and inconsequential to the personal pain and suffering you may experience during your recovery period. The cap on the personal injury benefit may not pay the medical care costs in full. How far does $25,000 or $50,000 go in your community? The income loss benefit of $300 to $800 per week will also be capped as to total amount and duration! This is no problem if you have a salary continuation plan. It's also not a problem if you have adequate individual long-term disability insurance. If the disability lasts more than ninety days or the duration of the salary continuation plan, will individual and group income replacement insurance benefits be sufficient to meet family financial obligations, including funding for retirement and potential increased cost of recovery?

Either your auto insurance or homeowners insurance will pay for your medical and recovery costs up to the specified limits stated in the policy. The driver of the car that hit you may be responsible for damages to your car or property and for medical care up to the limits of his or her auto policy if you were not found to be at fault. And, if you were a passenger in someone else's car, your auto/homeowners policy would pay most, if not all, of your medical and recovery costs, again, to the limits of your policy (unless the other driver was found to be at fault, in which case that driver's insurance would pay for the recovery up to its limit).

In each case, the limits of financial recovery may be exceeded by actual costs of care and recovery. Your only recourse would be to sue the at-fault driver for recovery of actual damages, pain and suffering damages, and attorney fees. Your attorney would sue the driver for recovery even if that required the at-fault driver to liquidate personal assets to pay the judgment, assuming you are successful in your suit. In addition to medical coverage and property coverage, the at-fault driver could further protect his or her net worth by purchasing a personal excess liability umbrella rider in the range of $1,000,000 to $5,000,000.

Let's assume that you have adequate income replacement for you and your family's well-being, that you are able to recover costs and damages from the at-fault driver, but that you do not recover well and are now disabled for more than one year. What about the practice? You may not fully recover and be unable to resume your practice. Your patients may seek care elsewhere or your partners may not be able to fulfill your obligations under managed care contracts. Valuable revenue contracts may be lost or compromised. Cash flow at the practice may be compromised. You may have no other choice but to cut costs. You could lose valued employees. You could lose valued employee benefits, further increasing the costs of damages from the car accident. Now that the disability lasted for twelve months, you may be required to sell your interest in the practice, not by choice but by employment contract. You could lose your practice! This is not a problem if you have business continuation coverage to include locum tenants and cash flow replacement to pay expenses.

Let's go with the probability that you will not be one of the unfortunate ones to suffer such a catastrophe. On the other hand, is it possible that you might throw your back out while golfing? Break your ankle playing tennis? Slip on the ice? Fall down the stairs? Get carpal tunnel syndrome from working on your computer? Have a sudden heart attack? Risk is all around us. Even though we may reduce certain risks, we cannot eliminate risk completely. The further difficulty with these other disabilities is the fact that there is no one to blame, to sue, or to recover damages from.

Your financial future is too important not to have as much income insurance as necessary and the most comprehensive coverage available. Most of us are aware of the necessity for medical coverage, but we often neglect disability insurance when determining our insurance needs. Disability insurance helps replace income lost because of an accident or illness.

Statistics show that for working individuals between the ages of thirty-five and sixty-five, three out of ten will become disabled for ninety days or longer, and almost one out of five will be disabled for five years or more before reaching age sixty-five.[1] Without disability insurance, that could spell financial disaster for you, your family, and your practice.

You have committed time, energy, and money to your profession and career in healthcare. Your ability to practice has provided you with an important source of income to maintain your present standard of living. Your ability to practice is your most important financial asset and it should be protected from loss due to disability.

Your present annual income, after practice expenses and individual income taxes, is important to consider as the base, minimum income replacement to maintain your present lifestyle, including funding retirement. Depending on your stage in the professional practice or personal life cycle, you may be

---

[1] *Life Association New,* February, 1997.

near the bottom or top of your specialty's income range. Anticipation of greater income in the future creates a larger asset to insure. Consider your current annual income multiplied by a reasonable annual increase, even if only at a minimum of the historic rate of inflation, multiplied by your remaining years of practice, assuming no disabilities or loss of income, and you will have calculated your future earnings potential. The future earnings potential is what's at risk!

At your current age, there is an actuarially calculated probability of chance of a disability lasting ninety days or longer before you reach the age of sixty-five. Your need is to protect your earning potential against this risk of disability.

Selecting the Right Coverage

How is *disability* defined? First, check the policy's definition of disability. Make sure the policy protects you against your inability to work in your present specialty-specific occupation. Otherwise, your insurer will not pay you unless you can't work at all. Are education, experience, and past earnings taken into account when determining whether the insured can resume practice? Many policies provide for an initial "own occupation" definition of disability for a specified period, after which a different definition of disability applies. Group long-term disability (LTD) insurance contracts limit own occupation periods to two, three, or five years. Group LTD is clearly not a substitute for a quality, individual policy with your own occupation and specialty protected to age sixty-five. Also, be sure to check the policy's definition of partial or residual disability benefits. Partial or residual disability benefits pay the proportional loss of income when the impairment allows the insured to perform only a portion of his or her duties or the disability reduces the insured's income by a certain amount from predisability levels. Purchase a policy that offers residual benefits. This will enable you to work for partial salary while you are recuperating and still receive partial benefits.

Next, make sure that you purchase a noncancelable contract that is guaranteed renewable to age sixty-five. With a noncancelable contract, the company must insure you as long as you pay the premiums. Your policy cannot be canceled for any other reason, and your premium cannot be raised.

You should be aware that certain provisions are included in most quality contracts. Some policies go "beyond the usual" and provide you with additional important provisions. And then there are a few quality contracts that go well beyond the usual and offer protection unique to healthcare professionals, beginning in school and protecting the individual with appropriate levels of coverage throughout his or her professional career.

So far, the usual contract provisions are noncancelable and guaranteed benefits renewable to age sixty-five, occupation and specialty-specific protection, and income protection for both total and partial income loss. The unusual includes future income protection, cost of living increases protection while receiving benefits, and coverage regardless of whether the source of disability was illness or injury.

Make sure that your policy makes cost-of-living adjustments. This will ensure that your benefits are adjusted for inflation so that they will still be worth what you need instead of being diminished by inflation. But more important, protect your future income. The future income protection agreement will allow you to increase your monthly benefit each year based on financial information only.

Finally, make sure that your policy doesn't differentiate between sickness and injury. It won't matter to your wallet whether you are unable to work because you're injured or because you're sick. Make sure your contract doesn't distinguish between these two types of disability and apply different waiting or elimination periods. Again, quality contracts will cover disability that results from an injury you sustained or from an illness that first manifested itself while the policy was in force. In addition, disability due to normal pregnancy should be covered after ninety days. Again, short-term salary continuation planning coordinated with the sick pay plan can protect the physician and employees from income loss in the first ninety days.

Another important point about disability income insurance is that it provides the ability to purchase future coverage, even if your health changes. There are special considerations for healthcare workers: Make sure that you have HIV positivity coverage in your contract—a provision that will protect you if you were to become HIV positive. The policy you are looking for must include presumptive total disability on diagnosis of HIV, and the disability period should begin at the discretion of the insured. Because of the unique needs of physicians, and in particular, the need to return to the practice as quickly as possible, some outstanding disability contracts provide full benefits until you are again earning more than 30% of your former income. When you earn more than 30%, you receive proportionate benefits until you are earning more than 85% of your former income.

Practice continuation insurance comes in the form of buy-sell disability insurance, which pays a lump sum sufficient for the remaining practitioners to purchase the disabled practitioner's interest in the practice, usually triggered at twelve months of total disability; practice continuation insurance, which provides needed cash flow to pay expenses, payroll, and benefits while you are incapacitated, including the hiring of an associate to attend to the patients' needs; and retirement disability replacement insurance, which pays the targeted retirement benefit or the monthly contribution necessary to achieve the targeted benefit.

The practice may also purchase life insurance on the life of the practitioner. The proceeds would be used to purchase the deceased practitioner's interest in the practice and would function much like 303 stock. However, the premiums are not ordinary business expenses to the practice and therefore are not deductible when paid. The proceeds are income tax free; however, the corporation must pay corporate income tax on the premiums.

WHY DO YOU NEED LIFE INSURANCE?

The purchase of life insurance is an option, *not* a requirement. It is a gift of love given for someone or something. Life insurance pays a death benefit to the beneficiary at the time of most need and at the time of greatest loss. The only requirement is that the owner must have an insurable interest in the insured. The insured, the practice or business, the spouse, the immediate family, and children have an insurable interest in the insured.

Depending on the age, health, and current insurable interest in the applicant, the amount applied for, and the type of policy (term, whole life, adjustable life, universal life, or variable life), the owner can provide needed cash at a present dollar discount.

The primary purpose of life insurance is to protect your dependents financially in the event of your death. Properly invested, the benefit from a life insurance policy can provide a steady stream of income for your family. It can also provide liquid capital to pay off estate taxes and other obligations.

How Much Life Insurance Do You Need?

The amount of life insurance is perhaps the most important question above all else. It is the question of love where all other questions are only financial decisions. This human life value concept is used extensively by economists in determining how much a surviving family should get if their family member should die due to negligence in a wrongful death suit. Typically, the human life value and the maximum amount that insurance companies will issue is roughly the same. The answer to this question is subject to how each individual feels about how much they would like to provide for those they love, which is a desire and not a need.

Some "needs analysis" life insurance calculations do not anticipate a family's changing needs after the death of the insured. These factors include technological, planned obsolescence, tax law changes, and others. Many calculations have been developed and debated to determine the absolute minimum amount someone should buy to provide enough money to generate a stream of income to the survivors of the family if something happens to the insured.

The Financial Profile Workbook will help you estimate how much disability and life insurance you'll need in order to provide your family with adequate income if you or your spouse should become disabled or die. A quick trip via the Internet will give you an interactive working copy (http://www.northstarfinancial.com).

Let's invent a fictitious couple, aged forty-five. They both work and have two children. On line 1, we've filled in the annual living costs for the dependents, including mortgage payments and other loans in this calculation. This comes to $170,000. If one spouse died, the income would drop off significantly. In this case, the surviving spouse's income is $60,000 per year. So, we've put that on line 2a. For purposes of this example, we'll assume that Social Security will provide another $20,500 per year. We've put that on line 2c, bringing their total available income to $80,500. Now we go to line 3 on the worksheet. By subtracting $80,500 from $170,000, we can see that this will leave the surviving spouse about $89,500 short. So, we wrote $89,500 on line 3. To estimate how much capital it will take to provide that income, we need to estimate the return they can expect on their investment portfolio. We'll say a hypothetical 7%. You can see that on line 4. Finally, we need to know what amount of principal or life insurance they can invest at 7% to generate an income of $89,500. So, we divide $89,500 by 7%, and we can see that they need $1,278,571 in life insurance.

DO YOU NEED PRACTICE INSURANCE?

Practice insurance is provided so that the practice and all the families dependent on that practice can continue to run smoothly if the physician/owner or key employee dies. With so many insurance product choices, how do you make an informed decision? First, you need to decide what type of insurance you want. There are two broad types of life insurance: term and permanent. And there are variations within each of these types.

Term Insurance

Term insurance is purchased for a specific period. When the term expires, you are no longer insured. Also, term insurance does not accumulate cash value. The entire premium pays for the death benefit. If the insured dies within the specified period covered, the insurance company will pay the beneficiaries the face value of the policy.

If your policy expires, you have the option to renew your coverage; however, you must pay a higher premium to do so.

Also, although term insurance generally costs less per year than permanent insurance for the same amount of coverage (i.e., it is initially "cheap"), the premium increases either annually or in steps as people age because each year the risk of death increases. Owning term insurance at this age can be very expensive and generally terminates before the insured dies (according to a study done at Indiana University, fewer than 1% of policies written result in death claims). At younger ages, term insurance can usually provide the same death benefit as other types of life insurance but at a much lower cost.

Permanent Insurance

The second general type of life insurance is permanent coverage. There are many forms of permanent coverage. Unlike term insurance, which is temporary coverage, permanent coverage can be kept in force until someone dies. Death is a certainty, not a possibility. Purchasing term insurance is like *renting* coverage; purchasing permanent coverage is like *owning* coverage.

Life insurance is an asset and can be purchased by many methods much like the purchase of a home. It can be purchased by a single payment, or it can be financed over fifteen or thirty years or more. Renting a house beginning at $500 per month with a 5% annual increase would entail a monthly payment in year thirty of $2,058 and result in $398,628 in total payments with *no* equity or tax advantages. The same is true when "renting" coverage.

When you purchase a whole life policy, you traditionally pay a fixed premium for as long as you live or for as long as you keep the policy in force. In addition to providing a death benefit, whole life insurance policies build cash value. Part of your premium goes to the insurance company for the pure protection element of your policy. The remainder is invested in the company's general investment portfolio. The insurance company will pay a fixed return on your cash value. This cash value buildup is part of the reason the premiums on a whole life policy generally remain fixed for the duration of the policy, instead of increasing to match the increased risk of death. As the cash value within your policy grows, the risk to the insurance company declines. Your stake represents an increasing share of the face value of the policy.

Life insurance can create an instant estate when you are young. Life insurance can preserve an estate with needed cash to pay estate taxes at the time of death. The value of your estate is simply the sum of all the wealth you have accumulated during your lifetime. This includes real estate, stocks, bonds, business interests, retirement plans such as 401(k), personal effects, and anything else you own. Subtract all of your liabilities on these assets or on your signature. The resulting statement is your net worth.

Estate planning, then, is the planning necessary to accomplish two goals. The first goal is to manage your estate during your lifetime. Wealth management is at the heart of a sound financial management program. The second goal is to make arrangements for the timely and cost-effective distribution of your estate upon your death.

One of the challenges in estate planning is estate taxes. When you pass away, the state and federal governments want a healthy piece of everything you leave behind. On large estates, federal estate taxes can go as high as 55%. Estate tax rates currently range between 37 and 55% of the gross estate. Having a life insurance policy that is self-supporting,[2] in that dividends are paying for the coverage, which was purchased for pennies on the dollar, is generally viewed as one of the most efficient means of covering these taxes.

If you are nearing retirement or are already retired, you have an entirely different set of concerns than those who have more time to accumulate their retirement funds. Let's look at some of the decisions you face at retirement. A couple with a $1,000,000 nest egg will typically spend only the interest on their money. Reasons include the following:

1. They do not want to outlive their money.
2. They do not want to become dependent on their children.

---

[2] If the nonguaranteed dividend scale decreases, additional out-of-pocket premiums could be required.

3. They do not want to become dependent on government assistance.

If current interest rates are paying 7%, this couple would be able to have $70,000 a year taxable during retirement without dipping into principal.

Instead, the sixty-five-year-old man could purchase an immediate annuity that would pay him more than $100,000 (50% tax-free) a year for as long as he lives, which would then be replaced at his death by the life insurance he purchased earlier in life. The net result would be a better lifestyle with more income and less worry for the insured during his retirement years with life insurance than without it. And the assets could be passed on to the people whom the insured loved most free of any income and estate taxes or probates.

Waiting until retirement to purchase insurance may be risky because the individual might not be insurable, and the coverage will be more costly than if the insured had purchased it at an earlier age. As discussed in Chapter 12, retirement is one area where procrastination can be particularly dangerous to your financial future and literally costs you money.

TAPPING THE HOME EQUITY MARKET!

Using the family home for a line of credit has become increasingly popular in recent years. Instead of refinancing the mortgage or selling the home, homeowners can receive a monthly payment for as long as they live, while still living in the home. Owning life insurance to replace the line of credit at death gives the family of the insured the option of retiring the debt or taking the cash income tax-free.

The next question that someone considering the purchase of life insurance should ask is whether they would like the flexibility to change the policy. Adjustable and universal policies allow the insured the ability to increase or decrease premium or face amount as life situation changes occur. This flexibility costs roughly 3 to 4% a year more than an inflexible plan. The cost for those who use this flexibility is generally recaptured after one or more changes are made to the insurance program.

With universal life insurance, you pay regular premiums to your insurance company. In exchange for these premiums, the insurance company will pay a specific benefit to your beneficiaries upon your death. Like whole life insurance, a portion of each premium goes to the insurance company to pay for the pure cost of insurance. The remainder is added to your cash value, which grows at rates that usually reflect current money market rates. Unlike traditional whole life insurance policies, universal life policies are very flexible. If your policy has sufficient cash value, you can vary the frequency and amount of the premium as you see fit. You can also increase or decrease the face amount of your policy to suit changes in your situation. If your financial situation improves significantly, you can increase your premiums and build up the cash value more rapidly. If you find yourself under a financial strain, you may be able to skip premium payments. In this case, they will be deducted from the cash value of your policy.

The next probable question to ask is related to flexibility. If an insured chooses to pay less than the minimum premium necessary to guarantee coverage no matter how long the insured lives, he or she may do so, but:

- Risk is transferred from the insurance company to the insured in that the company could require even higher premiums in the future than were initially set when the policy was purchased, or the death benefit could be reduced.
- Cash value will not grow as rapidly.
- Premiums could continue indefinitely.

The final question relates to where the dollars that are accruing in the policy are directed. Traditionally insurance companies invested primarily in long-term bonds and mortgages, which are thought to have less risk than securities. People who understand the historical risk versus the historical reward associated with the stock market and are comfortable with this type of variable return may wish to consider having the policy be "variable." This type of policy can also offer flexibility or "adjustability" in addition to being variable. Because the investments in the separate accounts require more management, the variable policy will cost slightly more than fixed products. In addition, there are not the same guarantees as with fixed products.

Variable universal life insurance policies operate much the same as "traditional" universal life policies. In exchange for a periodic premium, the insurance company provides a specific death benefit. The policies accumulate cash value on a tax-deferred basis. Like traditional universal life policies, variable universal life policies offer the flexibility to change either your premiums or death benefit to suit changes in your situation. But there is a unique difference. With a traditional universal life insurance policy, the insurance company directs the investment of your cash value. With a variable universal life insurance policy, you decide how the cash value is invested. The insurance company invests the cash value according to your wishes in a separate account made up of a variety of investment subaccounts.

This enables you to participate more directly in different opportunities in the financial markets. By directing how the cash value within your policy is invested in each of these divisions, you can be as aggressive or as conservative as you wish. The investment return and principal value of the variable subaccount options will fluctuate. Your cash value and your death benefit may be worth more or less than the original amount invested in the policy and will be determined by the underlying performance of the subaccounts chosen.

ARE YOU CONFUSED YET?

With so many questions and different products for various planning purposes, is it any wonder that people seek a professional to help guide them through the maze of choices? Up to this point, we have discussed only life insurance and related cash values as something that give the insured the ability to pay a level premium for life or a shorter period if a higher funding method is chosen. Many people also use insurance cash values to supplement retirement income. Unlike qualified plans, life insurance premiums are not currently tax deductible.

At retirement, there are three ways to access cash values:

1. Surrender the policy for the cash value. The gain (values minus the sum of premiums) will be taxed as ordinary income.

2. Withdraw cash values but keep the policy in force. This will still result in an income tax to the extent that cash withdrawn exceeds the sum of premiums.

3. Withdraw cash value equal to the sum of premiums and then take a loan on any desired excess value needed. The net loan rate equals approximately 2% per year, which in many cases is extremely favorable compared to paying tax on the excess. When the insured dies, the loan is paid off by the income tax-free death benefit. This technique is often used to provide tax-free income at retirement in addition to other savings vehicles that people *use*.

Remember that the most important thing to determine is the amount of money desired to leave a legacy to those you love. The rest of the discussion pales in comparison in terms of overall importance to the family unit.

PROFESSIONAL ERRORS AND OMISSIONS OR PROFESSIONAL LIABILITY OR PROFESSIONAL MALPRACTICE

Protecting yourself from claims of error or omission in professional judgment or treatment is essential coverage. The issue of "jointly and severably liability" puts you and your personal wealth at risk from the errors or omissions of others in your employ and other practitioners in your practice. Without discussing the merits of claims made versus claim occurrence contracts, the essential issues are single suit and aggregate limits sufficient to protect your net worth from judgments. First, look to your state's court cases for the highest judgment upheld on appeal in your specialty. The hospitals where you hold privileges may have already had this discussion with you. The highest judgment on record in your specialty in your state is the minimum single event coverage standard. Given the significant increase in awards, most hospitals will require you to show evidence of minimum coverage for $1,000,000/$3,000,000 limits. Working closely with your independent property/casualty specialists and your current carrier's underwriting specialist will provide quick analysis to your current coverage and recommendations for improved coverage. With this analysis in hand, your independent agent can best assist you in shopping the market for competitive bids.

EMPLOYER LIABILITY INSURANCE

Protecting the employer from claims of error or omission in employment practices is increasingly more risky. The employer has exposure in many areas, including hiring, orientation, supervision, performance review, retirement or dismissal, education on benefit choices, breaches of confidentiality and other breaches made by other employees, defense costs and attorney's fees in defense of claims brought against the employer or against an employee while in the employ and supervision of the employer, and certain defenses not provided under ERISA or COBRA or other federal or state laws and regulation. There is no indemnity insurance available for criminal conviction under Department of Labor regulations (ERISA, COBRA) or federal and state laws. However, civil penalties and beach of fiduciary duty can be indemnified under the special riders available from several quality property/casualty insurers.

STATUTORY EMPLOYEE BENEFITS

The services of an insurance professional specializing in property and casualty risk assessment and underwriting are required to adequately address the employer's exposures under worker's compensation. Federal and state laws and regulations are specific about compliance with withholding and reporting requirements. Federal and state unemployment taxes are capped and apply to first dollar payroll. Worker's compensation is purchased through the state pool, state fund mutual companies, or private insurers. Again, underwriting based on claims experience and risk exposure in your practice can result in substantial savings in premium. Ambulatory practices have considerably fewer back injuries than hospital or nursing home employees experience. Your practice has historically been rated at the lowest exposure rating and consequently, the best premium. The hospital and nursing home employees are rated at the top of the exposure ratings and incur the highest premium. Check your group's rating and address your claims exposure to premium costs. If you are compensated in any way through the hospital or other entity such as the health maintenance organization, preferred provider network or organization, or health system, check your group's rating against the larger employer's rating to again determine whether your practice is being excessively rated. Rates apply to first dollar payroll and extend to all payroll, including the owners' salary. The owners, being self-employed, may exclude themselves from worker's compensation under certain state laws, again, pointing to the need for individual long-term disability insurance.

The Timing and Types of Investment Vehicles

This chapter covers the basics—the "five fundamentals"—that every individual needs to know to be successful in achieving financial goals. There are no gimmicks to achieving wealth and financial security. Only time-proven fundamentals are covered. The five fundamentals are as follows:

1. Establish a "safety net" of cash and insurance.
2. Get started early and accumulate money systematically.
3. Minimize the impact of income taxes.
4. Use strategies that can reduce risk and enhance return.
5. Build a portfolio that matches your "personal profile."

As you can see, the first step is to establish a "safety net" of cash and insurance. The prudent man theory would have you hold this safety net in the most prudent account that would give access and assurance of return of principle. Protect your family and assets from loss of income or unexpected economic downturn by holding six months of income in a liquid asset account (i.e., money market account, savings, or your state's best municipal bond fund).

When we look at the combination the years of accumulation with compound interest, we are amazed at the results with only modest annual rate of return. This chapter explores the ways to minimize the impact of income taxes on your current income and investment returns. The dividend paid on your state's best municipal bond fund is free of both state and federal income tax.

This chapter also suggests that you use strategies that can reduce risk and enhance return. The most successful strategies are "dollar cost averaging" into "a well diversified portfolio of assets" comprised of cash or cash equivalents, bonds or fixed return contracts, and equities or stock, inside a "qualified account sponsored by your professional practice." The advantages of modern portfolio management in reducing risk and achieving desired returns are also discussed. Another successful strategy is, again, the dividend paid on your state's best municipal bond fund is free of both state and federal income tax.

And last, but certainly not least, this chapter discusses fundamental 5—how to build a portfolio that matches your "personal profile."

FUNDAMENTAL 1: ESTABLISH A SAFETY NET OF CASH AND INSURANCE

To get started, you should do the following:

- Insure to protect "human life value" and prevent other catastrophic losses. This includes home, auto, medical, and basic liability coverage to protect you in the event of a catastrophe.
- Build a "cash reserve" to meet short-term needs and emergencies (two to six months of living expenses in a safe, highly liquid account).

These measures establish a firm foundation so that you are free to make long-term investment choices that may involve risk and/or tie up your money for extended periods.

The big picture of this chapter is viewed as a pyramid with risk and return codependent, as the risk increases so does the likelihood of a higher return. In addition, the investment pyramid is built on a foundation of financial security from savings, health insurance, employment income loss protection, life insurance, and estate planning.

FUNDAMENTAL 2: GET STARTED EARLY AND ACCUMULATE MONEY SYSTEMATICALLY

There are two good reasons to start early and accumulate money systematically:

1. Starting early spreads the accumulation task over a longer period and enables your money to benefit from compounding.
2. Accumulating systematically breaks the task down into manageable amounts, introduces discipline in the accumulation program, and fosters a "pay yourself first" philosophy.

Even having this information, many clients will offer excuses regarding why they are not saving more now: "I'm just getting started," "I've got plenty of time yet," "I want to enjoy life today," "I've got too many bills," and "Social Security and my pension will take care of my retirement needs" are just a few examples. These excuses simply aren't good enough. Anybody can invest now. Here's how:

- Know where your money is going—do a cash-flow analysis.
- Accept that there is never a convenient time to invest.
- Determine a minimum percentage of your income you choose to save/invest (e.g., 10 or 20%).
- Target your accumulation goals and the amounts you need to set aside for each.
- "Pay yourself first"—in other words, *invest first* and *then* spend.

The cost of waiting, even a few years, has a dramatic effect on your ability to accumulate assets. Why? The dynamic power of compound interest.

FUNDAMENTAL 3: MINIMIZE THE IMPACT OF INCOME TAXES

Income taxes slow the wealth accumulation process by reducing your net return on investments. Although it is impossible to completely avoid income taxation, there are a number of ways to minimize the impact of state and federal income taxation. These include tax reduction strategies such as follows:

- Use the "qualified plan" options: profit sharing plans and 401(k) plan for for-profit entities, SIMPLE or SEPs for small employers, tax sheltered annuities and 403(b)(7) accounts for nonprofit entities, and individual retirement accounts if you do not qualify under an employer-sponsored plan or for your spouse if he or she is not covered by his or her employer's plan.

- Use annuities or your state's best municipal bond fund for nonqualified tax deferral.

- Generate tax-exempt income with municipal bonds.

- Focus on growth versus income investments.

- Invest in tax credit real estate.

- Match "passive" losses and gains.

The deferral of taxes on an investment can help grow assets faster, over time. It is important to remember that tax deferred is not, "tax-free." When the assets are withdrawn, they become taxable. If assets are withdrawn from the tax-deferred investment by a purchaser who has not reached fifty-nine and a half years of age, the full amount of assets withdrawn is subject to a 10% tax penalty plus current income taxes on all gains and principle. Let's take a look at how taxes and inflation can slow down the accumulation of wealth.

Taxes and inflation, when combined, can result in shrinking your total return. Over the long haul, bank savings accounts and CDs have not been the best place for your accumulation dollars. The investment is made with after-tax income; the risk of loss is low and therefore the return is low; and the interest earned is taxed as current income. Often, the after-tax return is less than inflation, resulting in loss of purchasing power. Larger sums must be put hard at work to build for your future and to help protect you against inflation.

Some investments are exempt from income taxes. However, the income derived from tax-free investments may be subject to state and local taxes and the alternative minimum tax. Typically, these investments are funded with federal, state, and local government bonds. To obtain the same yield in a taxable investment, you would need to achieve significantly greater returns, just to stay even with the taxed-exempt investment.

FUNDAMENTAL 4: USE STRATEGIES THAT CAN REDUCE RISK AND ENHANCE RETURN

When you allow your investment dollars to be exposed to investments that offer higher return potential, you increase your odds of wealth accumulation success. It's true that added risks are associated with higher return investments, but by putting some basic risk reduction strategies to work, investors can have the potential for the best of both worlds—a lesser degree of risk and higher return potential (Figure 14–1).

F I G U R E 14–1

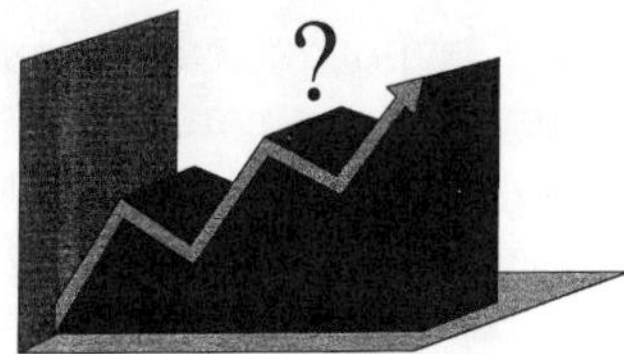

A $10,000 Investment in 1967 Would Have Grown To . . .

	Value - Dec. 31, 1997
Small Company Stocks	$ 362,960
Common Stocks	231,971
Corporate Bonds	113,233
Government Bonds	103,466
Treasury Bills	67,700

Past performance is no guarantee of future results.

The two biggest obstacles to investment success are (1) starting too late and (2) earning too little. The problem with earning too little is that it limits the power of compounding, you may fail to keep pace with inflation, and it is more difficult to achieve your investment goals.

As discussed in Chapter 12, there are numerous options for investments: money market (T-Bills), fixed income, and stocks. And although some investors see the stock market as a place to go to lose money, we have seen that having the fortitude and time to hold on to investments when they go down can be rewarded with gains in the future. There is a simple way to calculate the power of compounding that demonstrates vividly the importance of investment return.

The Rule of 72 allows an investor to determine the amount of time it would take to double the principal investment. This is done by dividing 72 by a fixed rate of return, which identifies the number of years it would take to double an investment.

Taken another step, the Rule of 115 allows an investor to determine the amount of time it would take to triple the principal investment. This is determined by dividing 115 by a fixed rate of return. The result is the number of years it would take for an investment to triple.

The Rule of 72 and the Rule of 115 are hypothetical rules and assume fixed rates of return over time without consideration of the value of the asset over time. There can be no assurance that these rates of return will be realized nor that the market interest rate relative to the fixed rate will not fluctuate over time. In addition, inflation, even at relatively low rates, can have a dramatic effect on your ability to accumulate wealth.

Consider that inflation, over the past thirty years, has eroded the purchasing power of the U.S. dollar by 79%. One 1967 dollar was worth only 21 cents in 1997, and slightly less than that today. Even with inflation at historic lows during 1998, the effects of inflation and the corresponding Consumer Price Index can be substantial to your wealth accumulation.

It is not enough just to preserve what you have now—you need to make your money grow, *just to stay even* with the rising cost of living. You can see why retirees on a "fixed income" feel the effects of inflation. Many don't seek higher returns on their money because of the following:

* They don't understand risks associated with lower returns of "insured" and guaranteed products.
* They have exaggerated fears of loss potential associated with potentially higher return products.
* They are more concerned with "not losing money" than with making money.
* Simple inertia.
* They do not know the prudent man theory from modern portfolio management," and consequently, they don't know where to find higher returns.

There are three basic areas to invest in: equity, fixed income investments, and money market investments. Virtually all investments are composed of one or some combination of these three. And indeed, ERISA section 404(c) on self-directed qualified retirement plan specifically refers to these categories as essential diversification minimums.

Equities

Ownership of equity in a business represents ownership of a financial or physical asset. The primary example is stock in a business. Stock may be preferred or common. However, equities also include real estate, oil and gas exploration, oil and gas reserves, and precious metals. All equities provide a major advantage over bonds in as much as they provide the opportunity of superior total returns over the contractual return of fixed instruments. Their disadvantages are that they have a high potential variability of total return, the principle may vary greatly in the short term, and all principle may be lost in the long run. Equities also need not generate dividends and therefore may not provide sufficient current income. In addition, they can be relatively illiquid.

Fixed Income Investments

Fixed income investments primarily consist of bonds or debt instruments, which represent loans to corporations or government entities. Bonds are short-term (overnight to three years), intermediate-term (three to fifteen years), or long-term contracts (fifteen to thirty years or more). Fixed income investments may include corporate bonds; municipal, state, or national bonds; mortgage backed securities; longer-term CDs; real estate contracts for deed; fixed annuities (loans to insurance companies); and the cash value of traditional life insurance policies.

The major advantages are higher current income than money market instruments, guaranteed return of principle with guaranteed current income (subject to default), lower investment risk than equity instruments, and significant potential for tax advantaged dividends. The disadvantages are that they have limited capital growth potential, they carry exposure to purchasing power risk, and they have moderate variability of return and fluctuation of principle as interest rates fluctuate.

Money Market Investments

Money market instruments consist primarily of very short-term debt instruments of commercial paper and government treasury bills and may include short-term savings accounts and CDs. The major advantages are they have the highest degree of safety, current income commensurate with risk, and maximum liquidity. The disadvantages are they have no capital growth potential, there is exposure to purchasing power risk, and they have a lower level of current income than can be obtained through investing in longer-term income instrument.

Being involved in the stock market means that you have to know when to buy, when to sell, or when to hold. Market timing requires that you buy low and sell high. You must always time the buy and sell correctly to win. If you are wrong on either end, the mistiming will negate gains and cause losses. Market timing can be an expensive strategy.

Implementing Fundamental 4: Adopt Proven Low-Risk Investment Strategies

The following are low-risk investment strategies:

- ◆ Emphasize "pooled products"
- ◆ Build from quality

- Use dollar cost averaging
- Invest long term
- Use asset allocation

Pooled Products: An Alternative to Direct Securities

Investments include investments such as mutual funds and annuities. They reduce investment risk through diversification, professional security selection and management, and access to dollar cost averaging.

Building from Quality

Remember the investment pyramid to build from quality and a sound foundation. A common sense approach to investing in any asset class is to start with a quality base, then to move to more aggressive investments. Too often, new investors have ignored this common sense approach.

Dollar Cost Averaging

Dollar cost averaging enables you to "buy low" and avoid investing at the top of the market. When you invest fixed sums of money at set intervals (e.g., weekly, monthly, quarterly), you are able to buy shares at an average cost less than the average price. Dollar cost averaging does not guarantee a profit or insure against loss in a declining market. Also, because such a program involves regular investment purchases regardless of fluctuation price levels of the investment, consider your financial ability to continue purchases through periods of low price levels.

Asset Allocation

Asset allocation may be used as a strategy to help minimize risk and enhance return. Allocation of investments may provide for an overall return that is greater than a single investment.

Some investments have a low correlation to each other. Simply put, correlation is a measure of how a particular asset will react to certain market conditions in relation to another investment. The classic example is that stocks and bonds tend to react differently to market events. By using both assets, which are not closely correlated, an investor can reduce risk.

FUNDAMENTAL 5: BUILD A PORTFOLIO THAT MATCHES YOUR "PERSONAL PROFILE"

The "best" portfolio for you could cause someone else to lose sleep at night. This process should take into account your personal goals and preferences, as well as an assessment of your existing holdings.

Some of you may be thinking that all of this information is a little overwhelming. And, you should know that you are not alone! But there is a process to getting started:

- Get the help of a financial services professional.
- Complete an inventory of current savings/investments.
- Discuss and put into writing your financial goals and other key "profile" factors.
- Select a suitable portfolio with the counsel of your financial services professional.
- Review and update the program at least annually.

After you have completed these start-up steps, you should be able to begin applying the five fundamentals to successful wealth accumulation.

How to Save Your Family Money through Proper Estate Planning

In the process of the professional and personal life cycle, estate planning becomes prudent to ensure that your wishes for your family and heirs are fulfilled and to protect your assets from unnecessary taxation and settlement costs. Regardless of size of the estate, estate planning is crucial. When someone dies, the survivors are often faced with many immediate problems. A long-term burden may also be created but can be avoided with proper planning now.

Estate planning determines the estate owner's goals with respect to his or her property during life, if incapacitated, and at death. The planning includes an inventory of a person's or couple's property by asset name, type, fair market value, and ownership. The planning process also includes recommendations for review and update of wills and trusts as well as arranging the estate owner's property to accomplish these goals.

Who needs estate planning? Who really needs estate planning? *You*—if you want to pass your assets on to your heirs in the most efficient, cost-effective manner you can. Passing your wealth on to the next generation has inherent costs. As your estate grows, these costs also grow. These costs can include estate and inheritance taxes, final expenses such as medical expenses and funeral expenses, probate fees, and accountant and attorney's fees, among others. These costs, especially the taxes, can be magnified if assets are improperly owned within your estate. Not only can improper ownership increase costs, but also it may provide an additional burden on your survivors because they don't have readily available cash.

Many people think estate costs take an equal share of both liquid and nonliquid assets. Estate expenses actually drain off liquid assets first. That is, those assets are readily convertible to cash.

Estate planning from a financial perspective focuses first on minimizing high estate settlement costs when possible. It then focuses on attempting to pay any unavoidable costs in the most efficient manner possible. Costs can be minimized by properly structuring your assets. And ownership of the right types of assets can efficiently pay unavoidable costs with discounted dollars while providing liquidity to the estate.

Estate planning provides liquidity for the family during the delay in settling an estate. Estate taxes are due nine months from date of death. Life insurance also provides liquidity to cover the unanticipated expenses.

One of the challenges in estate planning is estate tax. When you die, the state and federal governments want a healthy piece of everything you leave behind. On large estates, federal estate taxes can go as high as 55%.

Figure 15–1 shows the current federal estate and gift tax rates. Estate and gift taxes work in much the same way as the marginal tax brackets work with income taxes. Estate tax rates currently range between 37 and 55% of the gross estate. The implication is clear. If you have a sizable estate, the government wants to take a large share of it when you die.

Now, let's see how you would estimate your estate taxes. In our example, the estate worth $750,000 will pay federal estate taxes of $248,300. Fortunately, you would not have to pay this amount. The unified credit makes the first $600,000 of your estate exempt from federal estate taxes. The unified credit will increase through the year 2002 and will reach $1,200,000. Therefore, you are able to subtract $192,800 from the preliminary estate taxes. This leaves a total of $55,500 due in estate taxes.

FIGURE 14–1

Federal Estate & Gift Tax Rates*

| IF THE TAXABLE AMOUNT IS: | | | | |
OVER	BUT NOT OVER	THE TAX IS	PLUS	OF THE EXCESS OVER
$ 500,000	$ 750,000	$ 155,800	37%	$ 500,000
$ 750,000	$1,000,000	$ 248,300	39%	$ 750,000
$1,000,000	$1,250,000	$ 345,800	41%	$1,000,000
$1,250,000	$1,500,000	$ 448,300	43%	$1,250,000
$1,500,000	$2,000,000	$ 555,800	45%	$1,500,000
$2,000,000	$2,500,000	$ 780,800	49%	$2,000,000
$2,500,000	$3,000,000	$1,025,800	53%	$2,500,000
$3,000,000	—	$1,290,800	55%	$3,000,000

* Applies to estates of decendents dying after 1995.

NOTE: This is an abbreviated table, giving the most applicable tax brackets for affluent individuals.

Estate planning also deals with the problems encountered in attempting to transfer property to minors and to heirs who may not be financially responsible.

Estate planning deals not only with the financial aspects but also with the personal side. For example, providing for the care of minor children. A properly designed estate plan allows you to choose who you prefer to be guardian of any minor children and also provides for the proper management of your assets to care for your minor children.

Whether you like it or not, everyone has an estate plan. If it is not one that you have personally developed, your state attorney has developed one for you. If you do not plan your own estate, the state will do it for you. Here's an example of a typical state provided plan.

- ♦ Article I in effect says that you don't really care where your money goes. It's okay that all your money is split between your spouse and children and it's okay that they receive the money immediately.

- ◆ Article II of our state-provided plan might say that it's okay that all your money goes to your wife's or husband's new spouse and your children may not see any of it.
- ◆ Article III of this plan might say you don't really care who is the guardian of your children. Whomever the state chooses will be just fine.
- ◆ Article IV says you could really care less who handles your money when you are gone.
- ◆ Finally, Article V says that Uncle Sam can take as big of a slice of the pie as he wants. You don't mind one bit.

Most people will find fault with the state attorney's planning. So, now that you are going to plan your estate, what are some of the common mistakes that people make in attempting to develop an estate plan?

First, as we've discussed, many people haven't taken the time to even have a will drawn up. For those that have, that will is often left in a drawer somewhere and is never updated. If you have a written will, it should be periodically reviewed.

Second, the ownership of assets can be very important in minimizing the overall inheritance tax burden. If assets are improperly owned, you may be losing tax benefits that can be available with proper structuring.

Finally, in many instances, life insurance, typically the vehicle used to provide needed liquidity, is improperly owned subjecting it to additional estate and probate costs.

To avoid these mistakes, first, if you do not have a will, have one prepared. A will is the written document that sets forth your goals and desires as to how you want your estate handled and to whom you want your property to pass. If you do have a will, make sure that your attorney updates it periodically to take advantage of changing tax laws, but also to conform to changes in your financial situation over time. Another technique that can be used to meet your goals and objectives is to establish certain trusts. These trusts can be created both during your lifetime or may be created within your will itself. Trusts can be used to control the ultimate disposition of your property, even after you have been gone for some time.

The simple will, in a nutshell, leaves everything to the surviving spouse, then the surviving spouse has the ability to pass the entire estate to whomever he or she pleases. For example, let's assume the husband died first and the full estate of $1.2 million, in our example, passes to the wife. There are no taxes due at this time because of an unlimited marital deduction that allows property to pass between spouses with no gift or estate tax consequences. Following the wife's death, estate taxes will be due on property passing on to the children. From a tax perspective, this results in no inheritance tax at the first death, however, the *entire estate* is taxed at the second death.

Some advantages of a simple will are that it is easy to establish and all property can be left to the surviving spouse, whereas with no will, the children may get a piece of the estate outright at the first death. A major disadvantage of the simple will is that we may have increased estate taxes due after the second death.

Just a little estate planning can dramatically reduce the estate taxes. We could update the will in our example to include what is known as a unified credit bypass trust or a credit shelter trust. In this updated example, at the first death, the husband's estate is split: $600,000 going to the wife and $600,000 going to our bypass trust. The assets in the bypass trust can be used to provide income to the wife if she needs it, and the principal can also be used for the wife's benefit in this example should she need it. A provision of the law called the unified credit allows this $600,000 to pass ultimately to husband's heirs and incur no estate tax or inheritance tax whatsoever.

The $600,000 that was passed to the wife in our example can also be sheltered using her unified credit when she dies, resulting in no tax. In our updated example, the heirs received the full $1.2 million estate tax-free versus receiving just under $1 million because of the estate tax in our example of a simple will.

Another problem commonly seen in estate planning is life insurance that is not owned properly. That is, who is the insured, who is the owner, who pays the premium, and who is the beneficiary? For example, assume an individual has an estate of $4 million and part of that estate includes a $1 million life insurance policy. Estate taxes on that total including the life insurance are almost $2 million. Now, if we restructure the situation so that the life insurance is owned outside the estate, we can reduce our tax bill by approximately $500,000.

Other common estate planning strategies include outright gifts, grantor retained trusts, charitable trusts, irrevocable life insurance trusts, wait-and-see trusts, and family limited partnerships.

For example, take a husband and wife with five children. Each could give $10,000 to each of the five children, resulting in a reduction in the total size of the estate of $100,000 per year. Reducing the size of the estate also reduces the costs of transferring the smaller estate. This strategy allows you to give property away, yet retain its income for a given period. Because the beneficiaries do not receive this property until after that term expires, the amount of the gift may be only a fraction of its total value.

A second common technique is a grantor retained annuity trust. For example, assume your spouse transfers $1 million in stock to a grantor retained annuity trust. The terms of this trust allow your spouse to receive the income from that $1 million for 10 years. At the end of the 10-year period, the $1 million of stock will pass to her children. Because the children will not receive the $1 million for 10 years, the gift will be discounted from $1 million down to approximately $450,000. If your spouse lives for the full 10-year period, the $1 million in stock will be removed from the estate at a gift cost of only $450,000.

A third common technique is a charitable remainder trust. A charitable remainder trust is a technique very similar to the grantor retained annuity trust. However, at the end of the trust term, a charity receives the property rather than your children or other heirs. Using our example of $1million in stock, the stock would be transferred to the charitable remainder trust. Income from this trust could be retained by the donor or could even go to the donor and his or her spouse or even to the children. This income could last for a term of years or it could last for life. At the end of the term, the $1million in stock passes to the charity of your choosing.

Many individuals who use charitable remainder trusts wish to replace the assets that eventually pass to charity with other assets so that their heirs receive a similar amount that charity receives. The way to accomplish this is to set up a wealth replacement trust. The advantages of a charitable remainder with a wealth replacement trust are many. First, you've made a sizable gift to charity. Second, the assets in the charitable trust are not subject to federal estate taxation. Third, the charitable remainder trust will provide an income stream that you can use to live on and also to pay premiums in the wealth replacement trust. The amount passing to your heirs is preserved. The death proceeds in the wealth replacement trust are an attractive replacement for the assets given to charity. And finally, if properly established, the life insurance death benefit avoids federal estate taxation. The combination of a charitable remainder trust with the wealth replacement trust is a strategy providing many big benefits.

The irrevocable insurance trust is a common estate planning strategy. It can be used as just described as a wealth replacement trust or on its own to provide liquidity to help pay estate taxes. To establish an irrevocable life insurance trust, you would of course work with an attorney who would draft the trust document. After you've signed the trust, you contribute cash to it. The trustee will use the cash to purchase a life insurance policy on your life or on the joint lives of you and your spouse.

How does an insurance trust provide estate liquidity to help pay the estate taxes? The trust document has provisions the trustee must follow. After your death (or after both you and your spouse die, if the policy is on the two of you), the death proceeds are paid to the trust. The trustee can then *buy assets* from your estate *or make loans* to the estate to provide the necessary cash.

A new alternative to an irrevocable life insurance trust is called a wait-and-see trust. This trust is a "have your cake and eat it too!" strategy. You can own the policy today with a wait-and-see trust and still get the benefit of estate tax-free insurance later on.

With the wait-and-see trust, you own the policy today. Thus, you control its cash value and other benefits. Then, after you or your spouse dies (after the first death), the policy transfers to the bypass trust in the deceased spouse's will or to an irrevocable insurance trust. If set up correctly, the death benefit paid at the second death should not be subject to federal estate tax. Many married couples have considered using this wait-and-see trust as an alternative or in addition to the irrevocable insurance trust.

One other estate planning strategy that is currently very noteworthy is the family limited partnership. A family limited partnership is a good way for parents to transfer property to their children and still retain some control. The parents or senior generations are the "general partners." Or sometimes they own a corporation that is the general partner. In that case, because the parents own the corporation, the parents control the general partner.

The parents or senior generation establishes the family limited partnership. They transfer real estate, corporate stock, or other investments into the partnership. Usually, 1% or more of the partnership units are the general partnership units and the balance are limited partnership units. Initially, the parents own all the units of the partnership.

The parents, however, plan to transfer the limited partnership units to the next generation. So they make gifts to their children of the limited partnership interests. Under current law the parents can *discount* the value of these gifts because the gift is of a limited partnership interest. And because they are the general partners, the parents retain management control of the assets in the partnership.

We've covered many details about these various strategies in this book. All of these strategies are good ones, but how do you know which ones are right for you?

The first step in the process is to select your estate planning team. The last chapter of this book addresses these and other professional roles you may wish to consider for your team.

Next, list an inventory of your estate. You will need not only a current net worth statement, but an itemized list of assets and liabilities with owner and beneficiary identified by line item. Your financial planner, attorney, or accountant can work with you to put together a list of your assets.

Next, estimate what your estate expenses will be under various alternative plans. Seek advice from your advisory team that would provide you with creative alternatives that will work for you to help reduce those expenses. Your team will provide you with a written analysis, including recommendations on strategies that may be appropriate for you. Some of the strategies discussed in this chapter could be included in the recommendations. But again, it all depends on your unique situation.

By following these steps carefully, you can develop an estate plan that will meet your goals *and* provide benefits to your children and grandchildren.

How to Do a Financial Needs Assessment Using Selected Appropriate Consultants, Financial Planners, and Attorneys

Practice development, management, and financial planning are complex disciplines. Practice management and personal wealth accumulation planning are complex fields that cover many areas requiring special expertise, credentials, and licensures, including management, operations, human resource development, employee benefits, accounting, finance, risk management, insurance, business law, family law, and taxation. With the integrated factors of employee benefits, retirement benefits, and estate planning, the need for competent advisors dramatically increases. Effective and efficient practice management requires the efforts and collaboration of more than one professional.

Nonetheless, there is no substitute for professional management in the professional practice. Sometimes the accountant, the life agent, the investment advisor or others on your team may have special training in financial strategies. Few have the broader knowledge base to successfully help you coordinate the efforts of the team. Choosing a practice manager is also a complex process and outside the scope of this book. However, you may want to contact Medical Group Managers Association at their website (http://www.mgma.org) for help. As your practice environment grows and the complexities of administration increase, you will need to rely on the advice and council of other professionals.

The issues within practice and personal financial management have resulted in the interdisciplinary integration of various professions, including law, accounting, management, human resource management, employee benefits, and risk management. Given the complexities of financial planning process, personal as well as practice, and the interdisciplinary integration of various professions, the planning team approach may be your best approach to formulating and achieving your financial plan.

The practice and personal planning teams may consist of two or more of the following.

THE CHIEF EXECUTIVE OFFICER OF THE TEAM

You are the CEO of the team. You may share this responsibility with others in your practice as partners, board members, or officers in the practice. On the personal side, you share this responsibility with your spouse. You may delegate this authority to a nonphysician or nonowner in the practice; however, such delegation will not remove you from the responsibility of outcomes. You may delegate but not abdicate responsibility! You will make all of the final decisions after carefully reviewing the recommendations of the various members of your personal and practice advisory teams.

ESTATE AND PRACTICE PLANNING ATTORNEY

All practices require the services of a qualified, experienced attorney. Most attorneys can draft a will or establish a small corporation or partnership. However, it may be wise to choose one who specializes in healthcare as an industry. This is advisable whether seeking council in personal or practice matters.

Your personal attorney may specialize in family law or estate law. Regardless, your personal attorney represents you in your relations with the practice and in other matters of your personal life. Your personal attorney may council you on matters of your will, your estate plan, your employment agreement, your benefits, your real estate, and your personal matters. Your personal attorney represents you and not your practice!

The practice is represented by council to assure the owners on matters of compliance with state and federal laws as they apply to professional errors and omissions, the practice's operations, compliance with federal and state laws, employment practices, revenue contracts, facility and equipment leases, and all matters in business law. The attorney retained by the practice represents the practice interest and does not represent your personal interest. Unless you are the sole practitioner, not subject to jointly and severably liability issues, not a cosigner on any debt instruments or joint ownership of assets, you will be best served by retaining an estate planning attorney for your personal matters and a corporate attorney for the practice matters. Needless to say, it is wise to avoid conflicts of interest for your advisors. Be aware of whom the attorney was retained to represent and the experience, credentials, and skills required in that capacity. Your choice could mean the difference between the success of achieving your personal goals and the failure of your practice plan. Contact your state Bar Association.

CERTIFIED PUBLIC ACCOUNTANT (CPA)

All practices require the services of a qualified, experienced accountant. The CPA designation is awarded to persons who have passed rigorous examinations to demonstrate competency and who have been in practice for a number of years to demonstrate skills and experience. Depending on your stage in your professional life cycle, you may want to seek a CPA or firm that specializes or has associates that specialize in complex issues of practice valuations, practice formation and succession, practice revenue contracts, and practice overhead analysis specific to your specialty. In today's complex world of healthcare, the accountant you choose must have the knowledge, skill, experience, and a representable base of healthcare clients.

When your practice is well managed and you have maximized the benefits from the practice in forms of compensation and benefits, you have greatly reduced the complexities of your personal tax return. When you evaluate your personal net worth, you will list your ownership in your practice—your practice interest. In the event of a dispute with the IRS about the value of the practice interest, it will be prudent to possess a detailed appraisal prepared by a trained and qualified expert. This appraisal is valuable to you for estate planning, for calculation of your life and disability needs analysis and underwriting, and for practice succession planning. The CPA you choose for the practice may provide additional specialized services in personal tax matters and may be able to provide an additional objective overview of the financial planning process.

Choosing a CPA for your practice is based on different criteria than that used for choosing a CPA for your personal matters. However, the CPA chosen for the practice will be able to provide personal tax preparation and personal financial planning oversight as value added services. Again, your choice could mean the difference between successfully achieving your personal goals and the failure of your practice plan. Contact your state society of CPAs.

FINANCIAL SERVICES PROFESSIONAL

Financial services is a broad spectrum of needs and solutions analysis coupled with the use of suitable products, usually insurance contacts to sell off uncertain risk for certain premium costs, and investment products to meet retirement and employment benefits. There are several specialties you may consider in your practice as in your personal life.

Life and Health Underwriter

Health, disability, and life insurance play a significant role in personal and practice risk management. The bulk of employee benefits are funded through insurance contracts. Protection of your income, assets, and net worth is provided through appropriate and suitable insurance contracts. All states require *licensure* of anyone placing life, health, or disability contracts.

All insurance companies selling contacts in your state must file their contracts, rates, and experience with your state. All insurance companies must conduct background checks on their appointed agents and are held responsible for the conduct and statements made by its appointed agent as it relates to the insurance contract. Both agent and agency are regulated under the laws of your state.

Some life insurance underwriters have pursued additional studies in the complex areas of personal, pension, and business uses and risk management methods. Successful candidates earn the distinction of the Chartered Life Underwriter of CLU. A detailed view of this complex, but direly important, arena of financial services can be found on the Internet at http://www.nalu.org, home page for the National Association of Life Underwriters.

Likewise, some health and disability insurance underwriters have pursued additional training and studies. Because of the group purchasing of health coverage through the employer, most health and disability underwriting specialists pursue additional knowledge in the group benefits arena. Some professionals will hold the designation of registered employee benefits consultant (REBC) as well as the registered health underwriter (RHU) designation. A detailed view of this complex arena of financial services can be found on the Internet at http://www.nahu.org, home page for the National Association of Health Underwriters.

Property and Casualty Underwriter

Professional liability, general liability, and employer liability are insurable risks for you personally as well as in the practice. Worker's compensation is insured through a casualty contract. Auto, home, and general liabilities are insurable risks in the home. Personal excess liabilities umbrella is coverage provide through a property–casualty contract. *Separate licensure* is required in most states, and the license may restrict the holder to either commercial line of insurance, which includes facilities and professional liability, or personal lines of insurance, which includes auto, home, and the personal umbrella coverage.

A detailed view of this complex but direly important arena of financial services can be found on the Internet at http://www.rims.org, home page for the Risk and Insurance Management Society.

Some property–casualty professionals seek additional advanced underwriting knowledge and skills and have earned the designation of certified property–casualty underwriter (CPCU). Others can earn specialty designations in commercial property or personal lines. Again, the practice and you have different exposures and needs. Because of the overlay of the jointly and serverably liable issues in the practice, the nature of professional liability and employer liability in general, and the extraordinary need for personal umbrellas to cover excess exposed in all areas but professional liability, your property–casualty specialists must be able to advise you on all these issues.

Employee Benefits Consultants

Although some insurance professionals may seek the designation of registered employee benefits consultant (REBC) from the National Association of Health Underwriters, human resource and management professionals seek the certified employee benefit specialist (CEBS) designation from the International Society of CEBS. Again, the professional undertakes a rigorous course of study covering personal benefits and employee benefits, including health, life, disability, and retirement plans. The course work includes service needs and product solutions as well as the fundamentals of design, education, and administration of the benefit plans. The CEBS can be a valuable member of your advisory team if you are experiencing high employee turnover, increasing payroll costs, or redesigning your practice's benefits. Again, look for expertise in healthcare and the unique needs of individuals on the healthcare delivery team.

Retirement Plan Specialist

Many insurance and investment professionals focus on the qualified retirement plans, nonqualified deferred compensation plans, and after-tax investment needs of the individuals in the practice. Annuities, variable annuities, cash value life insurance contracts, and variable life insurance contacts are often used to fund these plans.

Professionals working with insurance contracts require a life insurance license. If the insurance contract offers subaccounts with investment options in addition to an indexed option, the professional must also hold a current securities license in the state where the client resides or is incorporated or has an office. Stock or bond brokers are licensed in general securities and must hold the series 7 license. The insurance professional may hold either the series 7 or the more restrictive series 6, which licenses the holder to trade only packaged products.

In addition to holding a license, either a series 6 (mutual funds) or series 7 (general securities), the licensee must be a registered representative of a broker–dealer under the National Association of Securities Dealers. The series 6 will limit the professional's advice to "packaged" products such as mutual funds and variable annuities. The series 7 is much more comprehensive in that its scope includes the underlying individual stocks and bonds that comprise the fund's holding as well as portfolios of individual stock and bonds. Both professionals with appropriate specialization can be valuable advisors to the design and implementation of the plans.

FIDUCIARY STANDARDS AND RESPONSIBILITIES

You are most likely a named fiduciary on your qualified plans; either as the owner of the practice, or as partner, or as a benefits committee or investment committee member. One of the most important functions and perhaps most onerous responsibility with all qualified employee and retirement plans is the fiduciary role. A fiduciary under ERISA can be held both civilly and criminally responsible for breach of fiduciary duties.

Section 3(21)(a) of ERISA defines a fiduciary with respect to a qualified plan to the extent he or she or they:

> exercises any discretionary authority or discretionary control respecting management of such plan or exercises any authority or control respecting management of its assets, renders investment advice for a fee or other compensation, direct or indirect, with respect

to any moneys or other property of such plan or, has any discretionary authority or discretionary responsibility in the administration of such plan.

Department of Labor (DOL) Regulation 2510.3–21 exempts a securities broker or dealer if that person transacts the purchase or sale of securities on behalf of the plan, in the ordinary course of doing business as a broker or dealer, if the plan fiduciary is not the broker or dealer and the broker or dealer is operating under written instruction from the plan. An insurance agent is similarly exempted if he or she provides the disclosure required in DOL Class Exemption 77–9.

Investment Advisor

Your investment advisor is a fiduciary under your plan and may be a named fiduciary in the filing of the plan and subsequent addendum and 5500 form filings. Except as noted previously. The investment advisor need not be licensed in insurance or securities. The investment advisor's credentials and methods of business are filed with the Securities and Exchange Commission (SEC) and may be filed with your state's Commissioner of Commerce, Securities, or Insurance. Some states require the investment advisor to pass the NASD series 65 examination before conducting business in their state. The series 65 examination is the only standardization in this arena. Regardless, the investment advisor is a crucial role that must be filled with a competent and skilled professional. Whether a needed advisor to the trustees of the plan or as your primary learning facilitator for the participants of the plan, the investment advisor provides valuable services and can reduce fiduciary liability exposure through his or her due diligence on the products recommended under the plan.

Financial Planner

The talents of a qualified financial planner can be an important factor in reaching your personal financial goals. The financial planner as employee benefits consultant and investment advisor to the trustees of the retirement plan can be an important addition to your management team.

Financial planners are not regulated in most states. Investment advisors, insurance agents, and securities brokers are. Professional boards regulate attorneys, accountants, and your profession, but few states regulate financial planners or those who call themselves financial planner, financial consultant, or the like. However, if a person holds himself or herself out as a financial planner for which he or she charges a fee for giving advice or for taking assets under management or accepts commission for any product he or she recommends, the person may be required to register as an investment advisor in the state in which the business is conducted. Also, if the planner has in excess of $25,000,000 under management, the planner will be required to register with the SEC.

Contact your state department of commerce or securities. A copy of the planner's business plan and credentials and, if the planner is a registered investment advisor under the SEC, a copy of the SEC filing and brochure will be on file.

You can find information about certified financial planners (CFPs) on the Internet at http://www.ibcfp.org. The International Association of Financial Planners (IAFP) also has information on the Internet at http://www.iafp.org.

GLOSSARY

Accreditation Certification by a nongovernmental accrediting organization that a given healthcare provider or service entity meets that organization's standards, e.g., the national Committee for Quality Assurance (NCQA) for managed care organizations, the Utilization Review Accreditation Commission (URAC) for utilization review organizations, the Joint Commission on Accreditation of Healthcare Organizations (JCAHO) for certain healthcare facilities.

Accreditation programs As employers and other purchasers of healthcare increasingly become concerned not only with quality of care, but with its affordability, an increasing number of provider organizations and health plans are going through accreditation programs to demonstrate their commitment to quality care and quality improvement.

Accrual The amount of money that is set aside to cover expenses. The accrual is the plan's best estimate of what those expenses are, and (for medical expenses) is based on a combination of data from the authorization system, the claims system, the lag studies, and the plan's prior history.

Actuarial assumptions The assumptions that an actuary uses in calculating the expected costs and revenues of the plan. Examples include utilization rates, age and gender of enrollees, cost for medical services, etc.

Actuary A person who mathematically analyzes and prices the risks associated with providing insurance coverage, or who calculates the costs of providing future benefits. An actuary uses claims experience along with underlying costs, administrative expenses, and anticipated investment return.

Adjustable premium Usually used in connection with guaranteed renewable health policies in which the premium is subject to change based on classes of insured.

Adjusted average per capita cost (AAPCC) The HCFA's best estimate of the amount of money it costs to care for Medicare recipients under fee-for-service Medicare in a given area.

Adjusted community rate (ACR) A rate-setting methodology used by managed care plans to set rates based on expected use of healthcare services by a group. ACR includes the normal profit of a for-profit HMO or competitive medical plan. The ACR may be equal to or lower than the average payment rate, but can never exceed it.

Administrative contract services (ACS) or administrative services only (ASO) contract A contract between an insurance company and a self-funded plan where the insurance company performs administrative services only and does not assume any risk. Services usually include claims processing, but may include other services such as actuarial analysis, utilization review, etc.

Adverse selection A population group in which there is an unexpected or disproportionately high percent of utilizers (or more intense utilizers) when compared with average or budgeted expectations.

Affiliated service group   A group of related companies, consisting of a service organization and other companies that have some degree of association and common ownership, that is treated as a single company for nondiscrimination purposes.

Age Discrimination in Employment Act of 1967 (ADEA)   As amended in 1978, ADEA requires employer with 20 or more employees to offer active employees above age 40 (and their spouses) the same health insurance coverage that is provided to younger employees.

Age/sex rating   A method of structuring capitation payments based on enrollee/membership age and sex.

Agency for Healthcare Policy and Research (AHCPR)   An agency of the U.S. Public Health Service, Department of Health & Human Services, that does scientific research, assessment of healthcare technologies, and support of clinical practice guideline development.

All-payor contract   An arrangement allowing for payment of health services delivered by a contracted provider regardless of product type (e.g., HMO, PPO, indemnity) or revenue source (e.g., premium or self-funded).

Allied health personnel   Specially trained and licensed (when necessary) health workers who perform tasks that must otherwise be performed by physicians, dentists, optometrists, podiatrists, and nurses. The term is sometimes used synonymously with paramedic personnel, such as physicians' assistants, and occupational, respiratory, and physical therapists.

Allowable costs   Charge for services rendered or supplies furnished by a healthcare provider that qualify as covered expenses.

Alternative Delivery System (ADS)   An alternative to the traditional fee-for-service healthcare system. ADSs integrate the financing of healthcare with providing patient care services. They may be in the form of an independent physicians association (IPA), health maintenance organization (HMO), preferred provider organization (PPO) or other managed care entity. Current trends have made these alternatives the norm in many urban markets. With insurers/payors moving toward prospective pricing methods, e.g., capitation, providers are adjusting to bearing greater risk and responsibility for appropriate resource allocation and usage.

Alternative dispute resolution (ADR)   Methods of resolving disputes, claims, and disagreements other than by the traditional method.

Ambulatory Patient Group (APG)   An outpatient case mix methodology that groups patient services and procedures on a weighted basis for purposes of fixing reimbursement.

American Association of Physician-Hospital Organizations (AAPHO)   Established in 1993 as a resource of PHOs. Address: AAPHO, P.O. Box 4913 Glen Allen, VA 23058-4913.

American Association of Preferred Provider Organizations (AAPPO)   A trade association of preferred provider organizations. Address: AAPPO, 1101 Connecticut Avenue, Suite 700, Washington, DC 20036.

American Managed Care and Review Association (AMCRA) A national trade association of managed care organizations such as HMOs, PPOs, individual practice associations, and utilization review organizations. Address: AMCRA, 1227 25th St. NW, Suite 610, Washington, DC 20037.

American Medical Peer Review Association (AMPRA) A national trade association representing federally designated professional and peer review organizations. Address: AMPRA, 810 First St. NE, Suite 410, Washington, DC 20002.

American with Disabilities Act (ADA) A law enacted in 1990 that prohibits discrimination against persons with disabilities in such areas as public accommodations and terms and conditions of employment.

Ambulatory setting An institutional health setting in which organized health services are provided on an outpatient basis, such as a surgery center, clinic, or other outpatient facility. Ambulatory care settings also may be mobile units of service, e.g., mobile mammography.

Ancillary services The services associated with services performed prior to and/or secondary to a significant procedure, such as lab work, x-rays, and anesthesia; or a charge in addition to the copayment that the member is required to pay, such as to a pharmacy for a prescription that has been dispensed in nonconformance with the plan's maximum allowable cost list.

Anti-dumping law A law that prohibits the transfer or discharge of patients for financial rather than medical reasons.

Antikickback law Sometimes used to refer to the Medicare fraud and abuse laws, which prohibit, among other things, paying or receiving kickbacks for referral of Medicare patients.

Any willing provider The law in several states that requires any organization dealing with medical services to admit any physician into the group who agrees to abide by the requirements of cost and quality.

Appropriateness review A utilization management technique used by third-party payors under which individual cases are reviewed for clinical appropriateness and medical necessity of surgical and diagnostic procedures.

Arbitration A method of resolving disputes without use of the courts. A single arbitrator or panel of arbitrators is chosen by the parties to hear the case, and the parties agree to be bound by the arbitrators' decision. The arbitrator's decision is usually final; a court will not overrule it unless there was fraud or partiality involved.

Assignment A statement, usually included on a claim form, that permits the insured to authorize the insurance company or health plan to pay benefits directly to the provider of the services.

At-risk-fee-for-service contracts Contracts that contain an element of risk because the contract specifies a withholding of payments to the provider by the HMO/PPO as a means for funding a risk pool. The funds in the pool are disbursed in whole or part by the HMO/PPO to the provider based on the outcome of goals for utilization of outpatient and/or inpatient services.

At-risk-fee-for-service revenue percentage   The percentage of total net medical revenue attributable to at-risk discounted fee-for-service contracts.

At-risk managed care   A managed care contract that contains an element of risk. There are two types of managed care contracts that may involve risk: (1) discounted fee-for-service and (2) capitation contracts.

Balance billing   The practice of billing a covered person for the difference between the provider's fee and the usual, customary, and reasonable (UCR) fee covered by the payor. This may or may not be appropriate, depending upon the contractual arrangements between the parties.

Base capitation   A stipulated dollar amount to cover the cost of healthcare per covered person, usually less mental health/substance abuse services, pharmacy, and administrative charges.

Basic health services   Benefits that all federally qualified HMOs must offer; defined under subpart A, section 110.102 of the federal HMO regulations.

Behavioral healthcare   Assessment and treatment of mental and/or psychoactive substance abuse disorders.

Benchmarking   Benchmarking is defined by the International Benchmarking Clearinghouse as "the practice of being humble enough to admit that someone else is better at something and wise enough to try to learn how to match and even surpass them at it." The two-year-old clearinghouse has grown rapidly and now has a membership numbering more than 260 organizations representing a broad range of industry.

Beneficiary   Any person, either a subscriber or a dependent, eligible for service under a health plan contract.

Benefit package   A collection of specific services or benefits that are covered by a managed care plan or insurance carrier.

Benefit year   A 12-month period that a group uses to administer its employee fringe benefits program. A majority of subscribers use a January through December benefit year. A benefit year, however, may not match the fiscal year used by a group.

Best clinical practice   Best clinical practice is developed with the process of clinically identifying the most appropriate and effective care for a specific condition and continuous improvement on that care using feedback mechanisms such as clinical outcome research.

Billed charges   A reimbursement arrangement under which fees for healthcare services are based on what the provider usually charges all patients for the particular services. Also called fee-for-service (FFS) reimbursement.

Board certified   Physicians who have successfully taken the examination of a medical specialty board.

Board eligible   Physicians who are eligible to take a specialty board examination as a result of completion of medical school and relevant residency.

Breakeven point   The HMO membership level at which total revenues and total costs are equal and therefore produces neither a net gain nor loss from operations.

Bundled billing   The practice of charging an all-inclusive package price or global fee for all medical services associated with selected procedures.

Cafeteria plan   A flexible benefits plan, generally one that complies with the requirements of IRC section 125 and offers a choice of two or more qualified benefits, or a choice between cash or one or more qualified benefits.

Capitation   A method of reimbursement whereby healthcare organizations receive a fixed per-member-per-month (PMPM) reimbursement for each of an employer's covered employees/dependents. The organization is then responsible for all medical services provided to those members.

Capitation contract revenue percentage   The percentage of total net medical revenue attributable to capitation contracts.

Carrier   An insurance company, a prepaid health plan, or a government agency that underwrites and/or administers a range of health benefits programs including, sometimes, delivery of healthcare services.

Carve out   A decision to purchase separately a service that is typically a part of an indemnity or HMO plan. Also sometimes referred to as single service plans (SSP).

Case management   A process whereby covered persons with specific healthcare needs are identified and a plan is developed that uses healthcare resources to achieve the optimum patient outcome in the most efficient, cost-effective manner. It typically integrates care provided by all the players—the payor, the provider, the patient, and the family—in an effort to find the most appropriate treatment for that person.

Case mix   The relative frequency and intensity of hospital admissions or services reflecting different needs and uses of hospital resources. Case mix can be measured based on patients' diagnoses or the severity of their illnesses, the utilization of services, and the characteristics of a hospital.

Case rate reimbursement   A contract in which the medical practice agrees to provide a medical service for a specific condition (usually specified by a specific diagnosis, or diagnostic related group (DRG) for a specified, fixed price.

Cash indemnity benefits   Sums that are paid to insureds for covered services and that require submission of a filed claim. Insureds may assign such payments directly to providers of services (hospitals, physicians, etc.). Payments may or may not fully reimburse insureds for costs incurred.

Catchment area   The geographic area from which an HMO draws its patients.

Centers of excellence (COE)   A network of healthcare facilities selected for specific services based on criteria such as experience, outcomes, quality, efficiency, and cost-effectiveness.

Certificate of authority (COA)   The state issued operating license for an HMO.

Certificate of coverage (COC)   A document provided to covered employees by the insurance carrier or managed care plan that outlines the benefits, covered services, and principal provision of the group health plan provided under contract by the insurer or managed care organization.

Certificate of need (CON)   The requirement that a healthcare organization obtain permission from an oversight agency before making changes. Federally qualified HMOs are exempt from having to obtain a CON.

Churning   A form of code gaming in which the same procedure is billed for more than once.

Civilian Health and Medical Program of the United States (CHAMPUS)   A health benefit program that provides coverage for armed forces personnel receiving care outside a military treatment facility.

Claims services only (CSO)   A CSO plan is a contract designed for fully self-insured employers that need very little administrative assistance. Under a CSO arrangement, the insurer administers only the claims portion of the plan.

Clinical/critical pathway team   Clinical/critical pathway team is a multidisciplinary team of generally 12 to 15 physician-directed, patient centered caregivers. The pathway of care and care team activities are directed toward a single diagnosis or group of diagnoses. The team follows a common plan that helps to provide continuity of care and decreases in variances of care that will lead to quality improvement.

Clinical practice guidelines   Clinical practice guidelines are patient care guidelines and algorithms that describe a range of diagnostic and management strategies for a particular medical condition or group of conditions. Guidelines are intended for use by a broad range of healthcare practitioners, including primary care physicians, specialists, nurse practitioners, and physician assistants.

Closed panel   The physicians whom members of a managed care plan are required to see because the plan has contracted with them to be on the panel; members cannot see physicians outside the panel of providers for routine care covered by the plan.

Coalition/cooperative/alliance/buying federation   A group of employers that organizes to have an expanded employee base and combined purchasing power for negotiating better contracts with providers and insurers. This also gives the coalition/alliance leverage to negotiate for improved access to information relating to medical costs, quality, and better clinical outcomes.

Coinsurance   The portion of healthcare costs for which the covered person has a financial responsibility, usually according to a fixed percentage. Often coinsurance applies after first meeting a deductible requirement.

Collective bargaining agreement   An agreement between an employer and the bargaining representative of its employees.

Community health information network (CHIN) A system to electronically link providers, payors, employers, and consumers in communities to improve healthcare quality and promote community wellness.

Community health purchasing alliance (CHPA) A purchaser of healthcare benefits on behalf of employer groups.

Community rating A rating method used by managed care health plans whereby premiums are set on a basis of anticipated average cost to provide services to any or all persons in a group or community regardless of factors such as age, sex, historical utilization, or current/previous health status.

Comorbidity Coexisting (usually chronic) conditions that may affect overall health and functional status beyond the effect(s) of the condition under consideration.

Competitive medical plan (CMP) A federal designation that allows a health plan to obtain eligibility to receive a Medicare risk contract without having to obtain qualification as an HMO. Requirements for eligibility are somewhat less restrictive than for an HMO.

Composite rate A uniform premium applicable to all eligibles in a subscriber group regardless of the number of claimed dependents. The rate is common among labor unions and large employer groups and usually does not require any contribution by the union member or employee.

Concurrent review A component of utilization management and quality assurance programs wherein admissions for hospitalization and subsequent stays are reviewed for medical necessity and appropriateness of care.

Consolidated Omnibus Budget Reconciliation Act (COBRA) A federal law that, among other things, requires employers to offer continued health insurance coverage for a certain length of time to certain employees and their beneficiaries whose group health insurance coverage has been terminated.

Continuing care retirement community (CCRC) A community which, in exchange for an entrance fee and a monthly charge, guarantees lifetime housing and nursing care as required.

Continuous improvement (CI) Using quality indicators to achieve certain levels a patient care services.

Continuum of care A range of clinical services provided to an individual or group, which may reflect treatment rendered during a single patient hospitalization or may include care for multiple conditions over a lifetime. The continuum provides a basis for analyzing quality, cost, and utilization over the long term.

Controlled group Two or more companies with a defined level of common ownership that are treated as a single company for coverage and nondiscrimination purposes.

Coordination of benefits (COB) A cost-control mechanism used by most insurers and managed care plans to avoid duplication of benefits.

Copayment   A cost-sharing dollar amount that an insured person pays out-of-pocket for medical services. Copayments are used to discourage overutilization of medical services.

Cost sharing   A general set of financing arrangements via deductibles, copayments and/or coinsurance in which a person covered by the health plan must pays some of the costs to receive care.

Cost-effectiveness   The degree to which a service or a medical treatment meets a specified goal at an acceptable cost and level of quality.

Cost/quality ratio   Cost and quality must be valued equally in the delivery of healthcare services. The four questions you may ask to evaluate the cost/quality ratio are (VanderVeen, 1988) (1) If the job was done right, was it done on time? (2) If it was done right and on time, was it cost-effective? (3) If it was done right, on time, and cost-effectively, were the desired outcomes achieved? (4) Is there another outcome that could be a quality outcome for this patient?

Critical pathways   Charts showing the key events that typically lead to the successful treatment of patients in a certain homogeneous population. They organize, sequence, and time the major interventions of nursing staff, physicians, and other departments for a particular case type, subset, or condition.

Current procedural terminology (CPT)   A list of medical services procedures performed by physicians and other providers. Each service and/or procedure is identified by its own unique 5-digit code. CPT has become one of the industry's standards for reporting of physician procedures and services.

Deductible   The up-front annual dollar amount that must be paid by the subscriber/member before insurance benefit coverage applies.

Dependents   Generally the spouse and children, as defined in a contract, of a person or subscriber covered by a health plan. Under some contracts, coverage may include parents and others.

Diagnosis related groups (DRGs)   A system used by Medicare for classification of inpatient hospital services based on principal diagnosis, secondary diagnosis, surgical procedures, age, sex, and presence of complications. This system of classification is used as a financing mechanism to reimburse hospitals and selected other providers for services rendered.

Direct contracting   Individual employers or business coalitions contract directly with providers for healthcare services with no HMO/PPO intermediary. This enables the employer to include in the plan the specific services preferred by their employees.

Direct contracting organization   A network established and owned by employers or a coalition of employers. A third party often is retained on a contractual basis to manage network operations. Also known as EPOs, or exclusive provider organizations.

Disability The inability to perform all or some portion of the duties of one's occupation or, alternatively, any occupation as a result of a physical or mental impairment.

Discharge planning A utilization management technique focusing on arranging for appropriate care after the patient is discharged from the hospital or other inpatient facility.

Discounted fee-for-service A contract in which the medical practice agrees to provide medical services to a defined population at rates that are discounted from full retail rates.

Disenrollment The process of termination of coverage. Voluntary termination would include a member quitting because he or she simply wants out. Involuntary termination would include leaving the plan because of changing jobs.

Drug formulary A listing of prescription medications that are preferred for use by the health plan and that will be dispensed through participating pharmacies to covered persons. This list is subject to periodic review and modification by the health plan. A plan that has adopted an open or voluntary formulary allows coverage for both formulary and nonformulary medications. A plan that has adopted a closed, select, or mandatory formulary limits coverage to those drugs in the formulary.

Drug utilization review (DUR) A quantitative evaluation of prescription drug use, physician prescribing patterns, or patient drug utilization to determine the appropriateness of drug therapy.

Dual choice Refers to the federal HMO regulation that requires employers with more than 25 employees who offer health insurance coverage to offer a federally qualified HMO plan as one of the health plan options.

Electronic data interchange (EDI) The computer-to-computer exchange of business or other information between organizations. The data may be in either a standardized or proprietary format.

Eligible individual An employee who meets the terms and conditions established by an employer, or its designee, to participate in an existing health benefits plan.

Employee assistance program (EAP) Services designed to assist employees, their family members, and employers in finding solutions for workplace and personal problems. Services may include assistance for family/marital concerns, legal or financial problems, elder care, child care, substance abuse, emotional/stress issues, violence in the workplace, sexual harassment, dealing with troubled employees, transition in the workplace, and other events that increase the rate of absenteeism or employee turnover, lower productivity, and other issues that impact an employer's financial success or employee relations management. EAPs also can provide the voluntary or mandatory access to behavioral health benefits through an integrated behavioral health program.

Employee Retirement Income Security Act (ERISA)   A federal law enacted in 1974 that allows self-funded plans to avoid paying premium taxes or comply with state mandated benefits, even when insurance companies and managed care plans must do so. Another provision requires that plans and insurance companies provide an explanation of benefits (EOB) statement to a member or covered insured in the event of a denial of a claim, explaining why a claim was denied and informing the individual of his or her rights of appeal.

Encounter   Face-to-face meetings between a covered person and a healthcare provider where services are provided or rendered. The number of encounters per member year is calculated as the total number of encounters per year/total number of members per year.

End-stage renal disease (ESRD)   Terminal kidney disease. Sufferers are eligible for Medicare benefits.

Enrollee   Any person eligible for services, either as a subscriber or a dependent, in accordance with a contract.

Episode of care   Treatment rendered in a defined time frame for a specific disease. Episodes provide a useful basis for analyzing quality, cost and utilization patterns.

Exclusions   Special conditions, e.g., preexisting conditions or circumstances in a group health plan that are not covered.

Exclusive provider organization (EPO)   A form of managed care plan, an EPO is similar to an HMO in that it uses primary care physicians as gatekeepers, often capitates providers, has a limited provider panel, and uses an authorization system. The main difference is that EPOs are generally regulated under insurance statutes rather than HMO regulations. EPOs are not allowed in many states that maintain that EPOs are really HMOs.

Experienced rating   A rating method by which factors such as age, sex, and health status are used to determine premiums. Experience rating places higher rates on those who have utilized, or probably will utilize, more services than the community average. Certain types of health plans are not allowed to use experience rating (e.g., federally qualified HMOs).

Explanation of benefits (EOB) statement   A statement mailed to a member or covered insured explaining how reimbursement was determined, why a claim was or was not paid, and the general appeal process.

Exploding   A form of code gaming. A billing practice in which the provider bills separately for each test performed on a given laboratory specimen.

Extended care facility   An institution that provides skilled nursing, intermediate, or custodial care.

Family and Medical Leave Act of 1993 (FMLA)   FMLA requires covered employers to provide up to 12 weeks of unpaid, job-protected leave to eligible employees for certain family and medical reasons, e.g., to care for the employee's child after birth, or placement for adoption or foster care; to care for the employee's spouse, son or daughter, or parent, who has a serious health condition or for a serious health condition that makes the employee unable to perform the employee's job. Employees are eligible if they have worked for a covered employer for at least one year, and for 1250 hours during the previous 12 months, and if there are at least 50 employees within 75 miles.

Favored nations discount   A contractual agreement between a provider and a payor stating that the provider will automatically provide the payor with the best discount it provides anyone else.

Federal Employee Health Benefits Program (FEHBP)   The program that provides health benefits to federal employees.

Federal qualification   The Health Maintenance Organization Act of 1973 encouraged the development of HMOs. Under this act, HMOs that voluntarily chose to comply with regulatory requirements more stringent than state law are eligible to receive federal grants and loans. The act also requires large employers to make HMO plans available to their employees if requested to do so by an HMO in the employer's location.

Fee-for-service   A traditional form of reimbursement in healthcare whereby reimbursement is made on the basis of the number of services rendered to the patient. The risk of patient services lies with the insurers/payors.

Fee maximum   The maximum amount a participating provider may be paid for a specific healthcare service provided to plan members under a specific contract. A comprehensive listing of fee maximums used to reimburse a physician and/or other provider on a fee-for-service basis is called a fee schedule.

Fee schedule   A listing of accepted fees or established allowance for specified medical procedures. As used in health plans, it usually represents the maximum amounts the program will pay for the specified procedures.

Fiduciary   Under ERISA, any person who exercises discretionary authority or control over a plan or plan assets. ERISA fiduciaries must comply with four general rules of conduct: the prudent person rule, the diversification rule, the adherence to plan documents rule, and discharge of his/her duties solely in the interest of the participants and beneficiaries.

File and use   A provision in the managed care laws of some states that allows a health plan to file for and immediately implement a change in an existing benefit without previously going through a protracted application and approval process.

Financial Accounting Standards Board (FASB)   An organization that establishes standards for accounting statements. Recently its attention has been focused on accounting for retiree healthcare liabilities.

First-dollar coverage   A feature of a healthcare plan in which the plan does not require its participants to pay any deductibles or copayments before benefits are received.

Fiscal intermediary An agency selected by healthcare providers to pay claims under Medicare.

Flexible benefits plan (flex plan) A plan that offers employees a choice among a number of alternative benefits.

Foundation for medical care An association of physicians that organizes and develops a management and fiscal structure and sets a fee schedule for individual physicians who join the foundation. Foundations usually market the plan to subscribers, provide peer review, arrange claims payments, and set rates for subscribers.

Full-time equivalent (FTE) The equivalent of one full-time employee. For example, two part-time employees are $\frac{1}{2}$ FTE each for a total of one FTE.

Gatekeeper A medical professional assigned responsibility for managing care on a prospective and concurrent basis. The gatekeeper is responsible for approving referrals and services prior to service delivery.

Global budgets Federal and state government set funding amounts that are used as the baseline to make spending and reimbursement decisions. The fixed spending budget is used to cover all healthcare activities.

Global fee A method of setting payment rates on an all-inclusive basis.

Government owned (GO) A medical practice owned by a government organization at the federal, state, or local level. Government funding is not a sufficient criterion for this category; government ownership is the key factor.

Grievance A member complaint against either a provider or the health plan. Health plans must investigate and resolve all grievances. Many plans require a periodic report of all member-provider grievances and a report on resolutions. Such reports must comply with specific grievance protocols that are normally attached as an exhibit to the master agreement.

Grievance procedure A formal process for the resolution of member or provider complaints, generally mandated by state law or federal qualification standards for HMOs.

Group Health Association of America, Inc. (GHAA) A trade association for HMOs. Address: GHAA, 1129 20th Street NW, Suite 600, Washington, DC 20036.

Group model HMO A healthcare model involving contracts with physicians organized as a partnership, professional corporation, or other association. The health plan compensates the medical group for contracted services at a negotiated rate, and that group is responsible for compensating its physicians and contracting with hospitals for care of their patients.

Group purchaser A person or organization that purchases healthcare services on behalf of an identified group of persons, regardless of whether the costs of coverage or services are paid for by the purchaser or by the persons receiving coverage or services.

Group without walls (GWW) A range of arrangements of physicians created to link them by sharing central services, form a unit for contracting purposes, and yet have autonomy by keeping their own offices. Also known as clinics without walls.

Guidelines Systematically developed statements on medical practice that assist a practitioner and a patient in making decisions about appropriate healthcare for specific medical conditions. Guidelines are frequently used to evaluate appropriateness and medical necessity of care. Terms used synonymously include practice parameters, standard treatment protocols, and clinical practice guidelines. Outcomes can be used as information to modify or improve guidelines.

Healthcare Financing Administration (HCFA) The federal agency responsible for administering Medicare and overseeing state administration of Medicaid. HCFA also manages HMO qualification and other utilization and quality review programs.

Healthcare Quality Improvement Act (HCQIA) A federal regulation that affords antitrust immunity for good faith peer review activities. The reporting requirement is mandatory to the National Practitioner Data Bank (NPDB) for settlements and acts involving licensure and medical staff actions involving a physician's status.

Health insuring organization (HIO) Usually an organization that contracts with a state or federal agency to ensure the delivery of services to beneficiaries of a state or federal program such as Medicaid or Medicare. The HIO will contract with health services organizations, either on a discounted fee-for-service or a capitated basis, for the provision of hospital and physician services.

Health maintenance organization (HMO) An organization responsible for providing or arranging the provision of comprehensive healthcare services, usually on a prepayment, e.g., capitated basis, to voluntarily enrolled persons within a designated population. Some HMOs emphasize prevention, wellness, and the gatekeeper model of primary care to maintain the health of their enrolled populations and lower costs.

Health plan A network of hospitals, doctors, clinics, and others, that provides a comprehensive range of health services.

HEDIS 2.0/2.5. Health Plan Employers Data Information A set of health plan performance measures that permits the trending of a specific health plan's data from year to year or compare measures among plans. Five major areas of performance are (1) quality of care, (2) access and patient satisfaction, (3) membership, (4) utilization, (5) descriptive information on health plan management.

Health promotion and prevention Process of providing information, fostering awareness, influencing attitudes, and identifying alternatives so that individuals can make informed choices and change their behavior to achieve an optimum level of physical and mental health.

Highly compensated employees (HCEs)   One of several definitions of employees who are not permitted to receive benefits disproportionately larger than other employees under the nondiscrimination rules applicable to employee benefits plans. As defined by IRC section 414(q), HCEs include 5% owners, employees who earned more than $75,000 (in 1991), the top paid 20% of employees who earned more than $50,000 (in 1991), and officers earning more than $45,000 (in 1991). Also called highly compensated individuals, highly compensated participants, and key employees.

High self-insured deductible (HSID)   Also known as shared funding, HSID is a way for employers to improve cash flow by self-funding the first tier of any employee's healthcare expenses. Employers can thus retain funds that would normally be paid to the insurance company to cover current and future claims.

Hospice   A facility or outpatient service program that provides palliative care for the terminally ill by relieving pain and providing counseling; a physician may elect a hospice benefit in lieu of more active intervention. The facility is typically licensed, certified, or otherwise authorized pursuant to the laws of the jurisdiction in which services are received.

Hospital affiliation   A contractual relationship between a health plan and one or more hospitals whereby the hospital provides the inpatient benefits offered by the health plan.

Hospital owned (HO)   A hospital owns the assets and incurs the liabilities of the medical practice.

Hybrid HMO   Known as second generation managed care systems, these organizations are extremely sophisticated in their organizational structures and product offerings. They tend to blur the differences among individual practice association model HMOs, PPOs, and managed care fee-for-service indemnity health plans; thus, hybrid HMOs offer open option or open ended products that modify the total lock-in of the traditional HMO enrollee to allow enrollees to use nonsystem providers but require a copayment, deductible, etc. These offerings are also known as triple or multiple option products. The objective of such products is to allow the hybrid HMO to more effectively compete with PPOs and traditional insurance programs.

Incentives   As related to health services delivery, this term refers to economic incentives for hospitals by means of third-party reimbursement formulas to motivate efficiency in management or economic incentives for physicians who encourage decreased hospital utilization, promote judicious use of all resources, and increase delivery of preventive health services.

Incurred but not reported (IBNR)   The amount of money that the plan had better accrue for medical expenses that it knows nothing about yet. These are medical expenses that the authorization system has not captured and for which claims have not yet hit the door. Unexpected IBNRs have been the major cause of financial insolvency for many managed care plans and providers.

Indemnify (indemnification) Protection or security against damages or loss designed to make whole the one sustaining the loss.

Indemnity An insurance program in which the insured person is reimbursed for covered expenses.

Independent living program (ILP) A program of housing assistance, job retraining, and other types of assistance to help disabled individuals live as independently as possible.

Individual practice association (IPA) A healthcare model that contracts with an entity, which in turn contracts with physicians, to provide healthcare services in return for a negotiated fee. Physicians continue in their existing individual or group practices and are compensated on a per capita, fee schedule, or fee-for-service basis.

Industry owned (IN) A medical practiced owned by a commercial business that provides medical services to the business's employees and their families as a means for controlling healthcare costs.

Integrated delivery system (IDS) A generic term referring to a combination of providers to deliver healthcare in an integrated way. Some models of integration include physician-hospital organization, a management service organization, group practice without walls, integrated provider organization, and medical foundation.

Integrated healthcare system (IHS) Combines physicians, hospitals, and other medical services to provide coordinated, continuing ambulatory and tertiary care to a defined population, often associated with a health plan, may also be called an integrated healthcare organization (IHO) or an integrated delivery system (IDS).

Integrated provider network A network of physicians, hospitals, and affiliated providers combined for purposes of sharing clinical and financial risk, while providing a wide array, if not total medical services.

International classification of diseases, 9th Edition (Clinical Modification) (ICD9CM) A listing of diagnoses and identifying codes used by physicians for reporting diagnoses of healthcare plan enrollees. The coding and terminology provide a uniform language that can accurately designate primary and secondary diagnoses and provide for reliable, consistent communications on claim forms.

Joint Commission on Accreditation of Healthcare Organizations (JCAHO) A private, not-for-profit organization that evaluates and accredits hospitals and other healthcare organizations providing home care, mental healthcare, ambulatory care, and long-term care services.

Kaizen   *Kaizen* is a Japanese term that means never-ending improvement. The American term for the same process is continuous improvement. The concept is to continually strive to make improvements in every area of an organization.

Lag factor   A general term indicating a percentage of medical claims incurred in a given accounting period but received, processed, and paid in specified months following the close of the accounting period.

Length of stay (LOS)   The number of days that a covered person stayed in an inpatient facility. Average length of stay (ALOS) measures the average length of time a patient is in the hospital.

Long-term care   Assistance and care for persons with chronic disabilities. Long-term care's goal is to help people with disabilities be as independent as possible; thus it is focused more on caring than on curing. Long-term care is needed by a person who requires help with the activities of daily living (ADLs) or who suffers from cognitive impairment.

Managed care   Form of health insurance coverage whereby enrollee utilization patterns and provider service patterns are monitored before (prospectively), during (concurrently), and after (retrospectively) the actual delivery of services. Managed care has the insurer playing a much more active role in determining what is done for an enrollee, where it will be done, who will do it, and what they pay for it. Many businesses have determined managed care to be an effective mechanism in controlling their healthcare costs. Managed care entities can be designed as PPOs, HMOs, IPAs, or alternative delivery systems/integrated provider networks.

Managed Health Care Association (MHCA)   A trade association of more than 120 major employees with an interest in managed care benefits. Address: 1225 I Street NW, Suite 300, Washington, DC 20005.

Management information system (MIS)   The common term for the computer hardware and software that provides the support for managing the plan.

Management services organization (MSO)   A legal entity that provides practice management, administrative, and support services to individual physicians or group practices. An MSO may be a direct subsidiary of a hospital or may be owned by investors.

Maximum allowable charge or cost (MAC)   The maximum, though not the minimum, that a vendor may charge for something. The term is most often used in pharmacy contracting; a related term, used in conjunction with professional fees is *fee maximum.*

Medicaid   A program of health insurance for eligible disabled and low-income persons, administered by the federal government and participating states. The program's costs are shared by the federal and state governments and paid for by general tax revenue.

Medical care evaluation (MCE)   A component of a quality assurance program that looks at the process of medical care.

Medical group practice   An organization consisting of at least three physicians providing healthcare services, which is formally organized as a legal entity in which business and clinical facilities, records, and personnel are shared.

Medical loss ratio   The ratio between the cost to deliver medical care and the amount of money that was taken in by a plan. Insurance companies often have a medical loss ratio of 96% or more; tightly managed HMOs may have medical loss ratios of 75% to 85%, although the overhead (or administrative cost ratio) is concomitantly higher. The medical loss ratio is dependent on the amount of money brought in as well as the cost of delivering care; thus, if the rates are too low, the ratio may be high, even though the actual cost of delivering care is not really out of line.

Medical Practice   An organization consisting of at least one physician or mid-level provider who delivers healthcare services.

Medical savings account   Employees choose specific dollar amounts on a before-tax basis to contribute to this account during the year. When an eligible expense has been incurred, the employee is reimbursed from the account. The IRS requires the employee to forfeit any contributions remaining in the account after the annual deadline.

Medicare   A nationwide, federally administered health insurance program that covers the cost of hospitalization, medical care, and some related services for eligible persons. Medicare has two parts. Part A covers inpatient costs. Medicare pays for pharmaceuticals provided in hospitals, but not for those provided in outpatient settings. Also called Supplementary Medical Insurance Program, Part B covers outpatient costs for Medicare patients.

Medicare HCPP   A healthcare prepayment plan contract between an HMO and the HCFA in which the HMO is retroactively paid for Part B Medicare costs. The HMO is not at risk for Part A or Part B costs.

Medicare Catastrophic Coverage Act of 1988 (MCCA)   A federal law that added significant coverage and substantially increased the cost of Medicare. The MCCA was repealed in 1989.

Medicare supplement policy   A policy guaranteeing that a health plan will pay a policyholder's coinsurance, deductible, and copayments and will provide additional health plan or non-Medicare coverage for services up to a predefined benefit limit. In essence, the policy pays for the portion of the cost of services not covered by Medicare. Also called Medigap or Medicare wrap.

Member months   The total of all months that each member was covered.

Morbidity   An actuarial determination of the incidence and severity of sicknesses and accidents in a well-defined class or classes of persons.

Mortality An actuarial determination of the death rate at each age as determined from prior experience. A mortality study shows the probability of death and survival at each age for a unit of population.

Multiple employer trust (MET) A mechanism that allows small employers in the same or a related industry to provide group insurance to their employees under a trust arrangement.

Multiple employer welfare arrangement (MEWA) An employee welfare benefit plan or other arrangement designed to provide benefits to employees of two or more employers that form an association for the purpose of purchasing group health insurance.

National Committee for Quality Assurance (NCQA) A not-for-profit organization that is widely recognized as the authority on quality for managed care organizations. NCQA's efforts in that regard are complimentary: evaluating the internal quality processes of health plans through accreditation reviews and developing measures and data quality verification capabilities. Address: NCQA, 1350 New York Avenue, Suite 700, Washington, DC 20005.

Network An arrangement of several delivery points affiliated with a managed care organization; an arrangement of HMOs using one common insuring mechanism; a broker organization that arranges with physician groups, carriers, payor agencies, consumer groups, and others for services to be provided to enrollees.

Network model HMO An HMO type in which the HMO contracts with more than one physician group, and may contract with single and multispecialty groups. The physician works out of his or her own office. The physician may share in utilization savings, but does not necessarily provide care exclusively for HMO members.

No-balance billing A provision in managed care agreements stipulating that the member, subscriber, or enrollee is not financially responsible and cannot be billed for any portion of covered services (other than applicable co-payments or deductibles) even if the health plan fails to pay.

Nondiscrimination The requirements in section 105(h) of the Internal Revenue Code (IRC) that self-funded employee benefits plans not provide significantly greater benefits to higher paid employees and owners than to lower paid employees. Although some disparity is permitted, there are limits which, if crossed, result in the benefits being deemed taxable income to the beneficiaries.

Office of Prepaid Healthcare (OPHC) The federal agency that oversees federal qualification and compliance for HMOs and eligibility for competitive medical plans.

Office of Personnel Management (OPM)   The federal agency that administers the Federal Employee Health Benefits Program. This is the agency that a managed care plan contracts with to provide coverage for federal employees.

Out-of-area coverage   Any benefits that a health plan will provide to its members who are outside the plan's service area. With rare exceptions, out of area coverage is limited to emergency services only. Out of area coverage is normally not the financial responsibility of capitated provider groups.

Out-of-pocket (OOP) maximum   The maximum amount that an insured employee will have to pay for covered expenses under the plan.

Outcome measurement   Outcome measurement is recording the outcomes/results of healthcare intervention. Measuring outcomes permits comparison to the original situation of the patient.

Outcome research   Research that is designed to identify and analyze the outcomes and costs of alternative interventions for a given clinical condition in order to determine the most appropriate and cost-effective means to prevent, diagnose, treat, or manage the condition, or in order to develop and test methods for reducing variations in care.

Outcome reporting   A way to score outcome survey questionnaires or other data collected from the patient care process, i.e., financial, institutional, or community related statistics usually done through a computer software program in-house or through a service bureau. There are several layers of outcomes data, i.e., (1) patient demographic data, i.e., treatment cost, social, key diagnosis, and length of stay (2) the patient satisfaction survey, (3) the health status questionnaires, and 4) comprehensive type forms directed to a specific diagnosis.

Open access (OA)   A self-referral arrangement allowing members to see participating providers for open panel specialty care without a referral from another doctor—typically found in an individual practice association HMO.

Open enrollment period   The period when an employee may change health plans, usually occurs once per year. A general rule is that most managed care plans will have around half of their membership up for open enrollment in the fall, for an effective date of January 1. A special form of open enrollment is still law in some states. This yearly open enrollment requires an HMO to accept any individual applicant for coverage, regardless of health status, and only charge them the standard community rate. Such special open enrollments occur for one month each year.

Open panel   A managed care plan that contracts with private physicians to deliver care in their own offices.

Out-of-area benefits   The scope of emergency benefits available to HMO members while temporarily outside their defined service areas. Some HMOs offer unlimited out-of-area emergency coverage. Others impose a stated maximum annual dollar benefit. Emergency coverage is usually the only HMO benefit in the total benefit package for which members may need to file claims forms for reimbursement of their out-of-pocket expenditures for care.

Outlier A person who varies significantly from other patients in the same DRG, such as a longer or shorter length of stay, death, leaving against medical advice, etc.

Outpatient A person who receives healthcare services without being admitted to a hospital.

Paid claims Measures what the carrier has paid, exclusive of employee cost sharing and provider discounts.

Part A The portion of Medicare that covers expenses incurred in hospitals, extended care facilities, hospices, etc.

Part B The portion of Medicare that covers physicians' services and other types of care not covered under Part A.

Partial disability A disability that prevents an employee from performing one or more, but not necessarily all, material duties of his or her job.

Participating provider A provider who has contracted with the health plan to provide medical services to covered persons. The provider may be a hospital, pharmacy, other facility, or a physician who has contractually accepted the terms and conditions set forth by the health plan.

Patient satisfaction surveys Patient satisfaction surveys are the scientific measurement of how patients feel about healthcare services and providers. The patient satisfaction survey now becomes a mainstream management tool for improvement and change in a healthcare delivery system. Techniques include nationally accepted surveys such as the Group Health Association of America's (GHAA's) protocol and survey form, monitoring of complaints, returns and customer service activities, focus groups, customer visits, warranty cards, standards, and indices.

Patient Self-Determination Act (PSDA) An act passed by the U.S. Congress in 1990 and which became effective in December 1991, which requires most hospitals, nursing homes, and other patient care institutions to ask all admitted patients whether they have made advance directives about the use of medical interventions for themselves in case of the loss of their own decision-making capacity. The institution is required to furnish each patient with written information about advance directives.

Payor Any individual or organization that pays for healthcare services including insurance companies and various government programs such as Medicare and Medicaid.

Peer review Evaluation of a physician's performance by other physicians, usually within the same geographic area and medical specialty.

Peer review organization (PRO) An entity established by the Tax Equity and Fiscal Responsibility Act of 1982 (TEFRA) to review quality of care and appropriateness of admissions, readmissions, and discharges for Medicare and Medicaid. These organizations are held responsible for maintaining and lowering admission rates, and reducing lengths of stay while insuring against inadequate treatment. Also known as professional standards review organization (PSRO).

Penetration The percentage of business that an HMO is able to capture in a particular subscriber group or in the market area as a whole.

Per diem reimbursement Reimbursement of an institution, usually a hospital, based on a set rate per day rather than on charges. Per diem reimbursement can be varied by service or be uniform regardless of intensity of services.

Per member per month (PMPM) Specifically applies to a revenue or cost for each enrolled member each month.

Per member per year (PMPY) The same as PMPM, but based on a year.

Percent of premium A reimbursement method whereby the provider receives a predetermined percentage of the insured's premium in exchange for providing all covered services.

Physician hospital organization (PHO) A PHO is a legally recognized structure formed between hospitals and physicians. PHOs integrate the clinical, financial, and administrative functions of both entities. The premise is that the PHO will provide the full range of services for purchasers of healthcare in a more cost-effective manner.

Physician network (PN) A network, IPA, or medical group that has entered into an agreement with a health plan to provide medical services to members.

Physician Payment Review Commission (PPRC) A bipartisan congressional advisory group established in 1986 to advise Congress on setting Medicare and Medicaid reimbursement. In 1990, PPRC's responsibilities were expanded to include other payment policy issues.

Physician practice management company (PPMC) An organization often a for-profit, stock company, which either acquires or contracts with physician practices to provide practice management services.

Physician profiling Statistical comparisons of physician practice patterns regarding such things as numbers of visits, numbers of referrals, numbers of laboratory tests, etc. The statistics are used to develop norms for identifying the most and least efficient providers.

Plan administration The management unit having responsibility to manage and control the health plan includes accounting, billing, personnel, marketing, legal services, purchasing, possible underwriting, management information, facilities maintenance, and servicing of accounts. This group normally contracts for medical services and hospital care.

Plan sponsorship The group that organizes the plan, finances its facilities, and/or makes up its governing board.

Point-of-service (POS) This product may also be called an open-ended HMO and offers a transition product incorporating features of both HMOs and PPOs. Beneficiaries are enrolled in an HMO, but have the option to go outside the network for an additional cost.

Policyholder Under a group purchase plan, the policyholder is the employer, labor union, or trustee to whom a group contract is issued and in whose name a policy is written. In a plan contracting directly with the individual or family, the policyholder is the individual to whom the contract is issued.

Practice management organization (PMO) An organization providing administrative, management, and related support services to one or more medical practices.

Preadmission review (PAR) A utilization review mechanism used by plans that utilize telephone-based nurses to review cases, assign expected lengths of stay, and issue an authorization number.

Preemption Overriding of state law by federal law, e.g., with certain exceptions, section 514(a) of ERISA preempts state laws that relate to employee benefits plans.

Preexisting condition (PEC) Any medical condition that has been diagnosed or treated within a specified period immediately preceding the covered person's effective date of coverage.

Preferred Provider Arrangement (PPA) Same as a PPO, but sometimes is used to refer to a somewhat less restrictive type of plan in which the payor makes the arrangement rather than the providers.

Preferred provider organization (PPO) Term applied to a variety of contractual relationships between hospitals, physicians, insurers, employers, and/or third-party administrators. In a PPO, individual providers or organizations negotiate with group purchasers to make available health services for a defined population. This arrangement typically shares the following three characteristics: (1) a negotiated system of payment for services that may include discounts from usual charges or ceilings imposed on charges, per diems, or per discharge reimbursement, (2) financial incentives for individual subscribers (insureds) to use contracting providers, usually in the form of reduced copayments and deductibles, broader coverage of services, or simplified claims processing, and 3) an extensive utilization review program of provider services.

Pregnancy Discrimination Act The PDA is an amendment to Title VII of the Civil Rights Act of 1964 that requires employers to treat pregnancy-related disability like any other form of disability.

Premium A prospectively determined rate that a member pays for specific health services. Generally, a comprehensive prepaid health plan will have a premium rate established for single members and for families.

Preventive health services Preventive health services have gained much attention over the last several years. Preventative service standards now require the development of specifications—clinical practice guidelines—for the use of preventive services by most accreditation organizations.

Primary care Provision of basic or general healthcare by primary care physicians, nurse practitioners, physician assistants, and other physician extenders. Primary care often emphasizes those medical services required to maintain good health or to treat simpler and more common diseases. Patients usually enter a medical care system when seeking primary care services and through a primary care gatekeeper physician in managed care situations.

Primary care physician (PCP)   A physician the majority of whose practice is devoted to internal medicine, family/general practice, and pediatrics.

Productivity   The relationship between output produced and input required to achieve that output. Productivity is usually expressed as a percentage describing the ratio between units of output to units of input.

Professional review organization (PRO)   A physician-sponsored organization charged with reviewing the services provided to patients. The purpose of the review is to determine if the services rendered are medically necessary; provided in accordance with professional criteria, norms, and standards, and provided in the appropriate setting.

Professional standards review organization (PSRO)   A 1972 law created 203 physician groups to review the care rendered to Medicare and Medicaid patients. The PSRO program was repealed in 1982 and replaced by the PRO program.

Prospective Payment Assessment Commission (ProPAC)   A federal commission established under the Social Security Act amendments of 1983 to advise and assist Congress and the Department of Health and Human Services in maintaining and updating the Medicare prospective payment system.

Protocol (algorithm)   A decision tree that describes a course of treatment or established practice patterns.

Provider   A physician, hospital, group practice, dentist, nursing home, home care agency, pharmacy, or any individual or group of individuals that provides a healthcare service.

Provider sponsored organizations (PSO)   A public or private entity meeting HCFA requirements that is established or organized and operated by a healthcare provider or group of affiliated healthcare providers. The affiliated providers share, directly or indirectly, substantial financial risk with respect to the provision of services and have at least a majority financial interest in the entity.

Quality   The features of a product or service that bear on its ability to satisfy the stated or implied needs of the user or consumer. Quality assessment should include consumers' evaluations of how well a product or service meets their needs and expectations with respect to process, outcomes, and perceived value.

Quality assessment   Quality assessment stresses the importance of quality measurements as the basis for continuous improvement in a healthcare delivery system. Quality assessment addresses (1) quality assurance, (2) utilization management, (3) credentialing, (4) preventative health services, (5) rights and responsibilities, (6) patient medical records.

Quality Assurance (QA)   A formal set of methods to measure quality of care.

RAPs   DRGs for radiologists, anesthesiologists, and pathologists used by the Healthcare Financing Administration to reimburse these specialists for care to Medicare recipients.

Reasonable and customary (R&C)   A term used to refer to the commonly charged or prevailing fees for health services within a geographic area. A fee is considered to be reasonable if it falls within the parameters of the average or commonly charged fee for the particular service within that specific community.

Reengineering   According to Michael Hammer and James Champy, authors of the book *Reengineering the Corporation*, reengineering a company means tossing aside old systems and starting over. It involves going back to the beginning and inventing a better way of doing work. It means asking this question: "If I were recreating this organization today, given what I know and given current technology, what would it look like?" Healthcare has gone through a macro reengineering process over the last five years through provider and health plan mergers, acquisitions, and reorganization. It is currently going through a micro reengineering process at the basic service unit level, e.g., the reorganization of the delivery of healthcare services to the patient.

Referral provider   A provider (usually a specialty physician or other health entity) that renders a service to a patient who has been sent to him or her by a participating provider in the health plan.

Reinsurance A type of protection purchased from insurance companies specializing in underwriting specific risks for a stipulated premium. Typical reinsurance risk coverages are: (1) individual stoploss, (2) aggregate stop-loss, (3) out-of-area, and (4) insolvency protection.

Reserves   A fiscal method of withholding a certain percentage of premiums to provide a fund for committed but undelivered healthcare and such uncertainties as higher hospital utilization levels than expected, overutilization of referrals, accidental catastrophes, and the like.

Resource based relative value scale (RBRVS)   A fee schedule introduced by the Healthcare Financing Administration to reimburse physicians' Medicare fees based on the amount of time, resources, and expertise expended in selected specific medical procedures. Adjustments are made for regional variations in rents, wages, and other geographical differences. Developed by Dr. William Hsiao and a Harvard research team, it divides Medicare treatments into 7000 procedures with specific RBRVS scales.

Retrospective review   Determination of medical necessity and/or appropriate billing practice for services already rendered.

Return-to-work program A program of rehabilitation, job modification, and monitoring to return disabled employees back to work as soon as possible.

Rider A legal document that modifies or amends the coverage of a standard insurance policy.

Risk The chain of possibility of loss. In insurance terms, it is the probability of loss associated with a given population. The term may also include physicians, who may be held at risk if hospitalization rates exceed agreed-upon thresholds. The sharing of risk is often employed as a utilization control mechanism within the HMO setting.

Risk management A program of activities designed to identify, evaluate, and take corrective action against risks of loss related to patient/employee injury, property damage, or financial loss.

Salary reduction agreement An agreement between an employee and employer to reduce the employee's taxable income. The amount of the reduction is generally applied to the employee's share of the cost of providing nontaxable benefits.

Section 89 A section of the Internal Revenue Code that set out certain written minimum requirements for welfare benefits plans to meet, as well as established highly specific nondiscrimination requirements. Section 89 was repealed in 1989 restoring the applicability of the nondiscrimination rules of IRC section 105(h).

Section 125 Plan A term used to refer to flexible benefit plans. The reference derives from the section of the IRS code that defines such plans and stipulates that employee contributions to such plans may be made with pretax dollars.

Self-insured The arrangement whereby an employer agrees to accept the financial risk related to providing healthcare to its employees and dependents (versus an insured program where a third party such as an HMO agrees to accept the risk for a fee or premium).

Senior health plan A plan for Medicare-eligible persons sponsored by an HMO pursuant to a contract between the HMO and the HCFA.

Service area The geographic area in which a health plan is licensed by a state to market its healthcare program and in which members must reside or work.

Severity of illness A measure of the intensity or complexity of illness, often in conjunction with other preexisting conditions, usually estimated at the time of admission. It is often used when adjusting the outcomes of care to the sickness of the patient on admission. Some of the measures relate to the likelihood of death, some to of loss or impairment of function, some to clinical efficiency of care (resources used per case), others to more abstract concepts.

Simple service plans   A free-standing healthcare program offering a single service, often created as a carve-out" and run by a third-party administrator. Typical single service plans include mental health, dental, or vision care.

Single specialty (SS)   A medical practice type that focuses its clinical work in one specialty. The determining factor for classifying the type of specialty should be the focus of clinical work and not necessarily the specialties of the physicians in the practice.

Sixth Omnibus Reconciliation Act of 1985 (OBRA/SOBRA)   Portions of this act created quality review organizations (QROs) and empowered QROs and peer review organizations (PROs) to monitor quality of care for Medicare recipients enrolled in HMOs or competitive medical plans, provided for civil monetary penalties for plans that failed to provide proper care, and restricted the types of physician incentives that a managed care plan may use when providing care for Medicare recipients. Also, the act made disenrollment from HMOs and competitive medical plans far easier for Medicare recipients.

Skilled nursing facility (SNF)   A facility that provides health and social services to patients on a less than acute basis when ongoing skilled care is required. These are commonly referred to as nursing homes.

Staff model HMO   A healthcare model that employs physicians to provide healthcare to its members. All premiums and other revenues accrue to the HMO, which compensates physicians by salary and incentive programs.

Standard benefit package   A specified set of minimum medical benefits available to all persons.

Short-term disability (STD)   A temporary period of disability usually not exceeding six months.

Stop-loss insurance   Insurance coverage taken out by a health plan or self-funded employer to provide protection from losses resulting from claims greater than a specific dollar amount per covered person per year.

Subacute   A level of care for patients who do not require the intensity of services of a hospital but typically require some support services.

Subrogation   The contractual right of a health plan to recover payments made to a member for healthcare costs after that member has received such payment for damages in a legal action.

Subscriber   An employer, union, or association that contracts with an HMO for its prepaid healthcare plan, which is offered to eligible enrollees.

Superbill   A modified claim form that lists specific and/or specialty medical services provided by physicians. It does not substitute for claim forms required under most managed care plans.

Supplemental benefits rider   A document showing covered ancillary services (e.g., eyeglasses or contact lenses), and which may be attached to the subscriber group contract.

Tax Equity and Fiscal Responsibility Act of 1982   The federal law that created the current risk and cost contract provisions under which health plans contract with the Healthcare Financing Administration, and that defined the primary and secondary coverage responsibilities of the Medicare program.

Technical and Miscellaneous Revenue Act of 1988 (TAMRA)   A federal law that revised the Section 89 nondiscrimination rules and amended the penalties for noncompliance with COBRA.

Tertiary care   Those healthcare services provided by highly specialized providers such as thoracic surgeons and intensive care units. These services often require highly sophisticated technologies and facilities.

Third-party administrator (TPA)   An independent person or corporate entity that administers group benefits, claims, and administration for a self-insured company/group. A TPA does not underwrite the risk.

Tiered rates   A multilevel alternative to blended capitation rates. Capitation is occasionally quoted on a two- or three-tier basis. If two tier, rates are for subscriber and subscriber plus family. If three tier, rates are for subscriber, subscriber plus one, and subscriber plus family.

Tolerable loss ratio (TLR)   The loss ratio the insurer can fund without losing money on the group.

Total quality management (TQM)   Total quality management is a way of providing services. TQM redefines quality by incorporating such factors as customers, suppliers, cost, continuous improvement, and price. Generally, TQM is a way of running and managing an organization that recognizes the customers/patients and the employees in adding value to the organization.

Triage   The classification of sick or injured persons according to severity in order to direct care and ensure the efficient use of medical and nursing staff and facilities.

Triple option   Multiple option plans that typically include indemnity, PPO, and HMO plans through one insurer. Triple option plans, in theory, prevent adverse selection by placing all employees in a single risk pool.

Unbundling   Separately packaged units that might otherwise be packaged together. For claims processing, this includes providers billing separately for healthcare services that might be combined according to industry standards or commonly accepted coding practices.

Underwriting   Refers to bearing the risk for something, e.g., a policy is underwritten by an insurance company. May also refer to the analysis of a group that is done to determine rates or to determine if the group should be offered coverage at all.

Uniform Billing Code of 1992 (UB92)   A revised version of the UB82, a federal directive requiring hospitals to follow specific billing procedures, itemizing all services included and billed for on each invoice.

Uniform clinical data set (UCDS) A computerized system to assist professional and peer review organizations in collecting medical record data and identifying cases with potential utilization or quality problems.

Union sponsored plan A program of health benefits developed by a union. The union may operate the program directly or may contract for benefits. Funds to finance the benefits are usually paid from a welfare fund that receives its income from employer contributions, employer and union member contributions, or union members alone.

Unrelated business income Earnings from actives that do not relate to an organization's tax-exempt purpose. Such earnings are taxable.

Upcoding In claims submission, using a higher level procedure code than the level of service actually provided.

Utilization management Utilization management is a keystone to effective healthcare management and is an important determination in both the cost and quality in a managed care organization. Appropriate utilization protocols and standards should be based on reasonable scientific evidence. Good utilization management system monitors for under-utilization as well as over-utilization.

Utilization Review Accreditation Commission (URAC) An independent accreditation organization for utilization review organizations with a goal of encouraging effective and efficient UR processes and providing a method of evaluation and accreditation for UR programs. Address: URAC, 1130 Connecticut Avenue NW, Suite 450, Washington, DC 20036.

Voluntary Employees Beneficiary Association (VEBA) Also known as a section 501(c)(9) trust with reference to IRC, a VEBA is a means of accumulating tax-free income producing reserves for life, sick, accident, or other benefits. They were initially formed and funded by employees, but changes in the law have allowed them to be used as an employee benefits vehicle by employers.

Waiting Period The period of time between an employee's hire and his or her enrollment in an insurance program.

Welfare Fund A fund into which employer and/or employee contributions for healthcare are placed and that is administered by a board, usually with equal representation from labor and management. When the welfare fund provides health benefits, it provides service benefits.

Withhold A percentage of payment to the provider held back by the HMO until the cost of referral or hospital services has been determined. Physicians exceeding the amount determined as appropriate by the HMO lose the amount held back. The amount of withhold returned depends on individual utilization by the gatekeeper; referral patterns through the year by the gatekeeper, groups of physicians or the overall plan pool; and financial indicators for the overall capitated plan.

Workers' compensation A state-governed system designed to address work-related injuries. Under the system, employers assume the cost of medical treatment and wage losses arising from a worker's job-related injury or disease, regardless of who is at fault. In return, employees give up the right to sue employers, even if injuries stem from employer negligence.

Wraparound plan Commonly used to refer to insurance or health plan coverage for copayments and deductibles that are not covered under a member's base plan. This is often used for Medicare.

ABOUT THE AUTHORS

As Vice President of Healthcare Consulting for Endurant Business Solutions, St. Paul, Minnesota, **John F. McCally**, consults with healthcare providers and medical organizations throughout the United States in the areas of financial management, operations improvement, managed care, governance, and strategic planning. With extensive managed care experience in markets throughout the country, he also advises providers regarding their managed care contracting and strategic positioning.

Prior to this position, Mr. McCally served as the National Director of Health Care Reform with McGladrey & Pullen for four years and spent three years as senior advisor for Medical Group consulting for Ernst & Young, both national accounting and consulting firms. Mr. McCally also has extensive experience as a senior healthcare executive and CEO, having served numerous and diverse healthcare organizations, such as the Detroit Medical Center and the Mayo Clinic, and being a hospital administrator of an all computerized hospital for American Medical International.

Mr. McCally is a nationally recognized speaker and has published more than 50 articles and books on managed care, healthcare system change, and strategic planning. His most recent book with McGraw-Hill Healthcare Education Group was *Physician Practice Management Redefined* (1998). Mr. McCally is a member of the Medical Group Management Association, National Health Lawyers Association, and American College of Medical Quality. He also serves as an adjunct faculty member of the Carlson School of Management at the University of Minnesota.

Paul A. Wilkus is President of Health Financial Group, Inc., fee-for-service financial planners, investment advisors, and risk management consultants located in Minneapolis. As financial consultant to healthcare providers and a former medical group administrator, Mr. Wilkus has demonstrated abilities in the development and management of health care practices. He specializes in the employer-employee relationship in the areas of professional compensation and benefits, individual and group financial planning, practice valuations, estate and retirement planning. Mr. Wilkus has written and lectured on topics germane to healthcare, its delivery, and its finance since 1974.

Mr. Wilkus is a 1974 graduate of the University of Minnesota and has degrees in Business Administration with concentrations in finance and accounting, and Philosophy with concentrations in law, ethics, and social contract.

Mr. Wilkus is a member of Minnesota Medical Group Managers Association, Minnesota Association of Life Underwriters, Minnesota Association of Health Underwriters, Past Board Member and Ethics Officer (1990–1994) for the state chapter of the International Association of Financial Planners, a Registered Financial Consultant, and lecturer in risk management and financial services at the Carlson School of Management, University of Minnesota. Paul has spoken to numerous state and county medical and dental societies on issues in financial planning and risk management in professional practices.

I N D E X